Martha Everts Holden

Rosemary and Rue

Martha Everts Holden

Rosemary and Rue

ISBN/EAN: 9783742812421

Manufactured in Europe, USA, Canada, Australia, Japa

Cover: Foto ©Andreas Hilbeck / pixelio.de

Manufactured and distributed by brebook publishing software (www.brebook.com)

Martha Everts Holden

Rosemary and Rue

Rosemary and Rue

By Amber

Chicago and New York:
Rand, McNally & Company,
MDCCCXCVII.

Copyright, 1896, by Rand, McNally & Co.

PREFACE.

"Amber" was not to be classed with any society or any creed. In all respects she was an individual. In good-humored contempt she held all form, and with deep sincerity she revered all simple things. She smiled upon error and frowned upon pretense. Her life was largely made up of impulse and sacrifice. She was the constant "victim" of her own generosity, needing the money and the time which sympathy impelled her to give away. She was so devoted a lover of the moods of nature, noting so closely the changing of the leaf or a new note sounded by the whimsical wind, that her spirit itself must once have been an October day. Year after year she toiled, and her reward was not money, but a letter from the bedside of the invalid, telling of a heart that had been lightened, of a care that had been driven from the door. None of the newspaper writers of Chicago was more popular. Another column told the news of the day; her column held the news of the heart. Her best thoughts and warmest fancies are scattered throughout her prose. Her verses are pleasant, and many of them are striking, but meter often chained her fancy. But some of her unchained fancies, poetic conceits in the guise of prose, will live long after the clasp, holding the pretentious verses of a society laureate, shall have been eaten loose by the constant nibble of time.

When a church was crowded with friends, come to bid "Amber" good-bye, a great thinker, a writer who knows the meaning of toil, said that she had succeeded by the force and the industry of her genius. And so she had. For others, influence searched out easy places, but "Amber" found her own hard place and maintained it, struggling alone. Her words were for the poor and the sorrowful, and they could but give a blessing. But in the end, a blessing from the poor may be brighter than the silver of the rich. Opie Read.

Rosemary and Rue.

I WONDER.

I wonder, if I died to-night,
  And you should hear to-morrow,
You'd mourn to think this one dear friend
  Had bid good-bye to sorrow.

I wonder, if you saw a bird,
  The hunter's dart outflying,
You'd lure it back with loving word
  To danger, pain, and dying.

I wonder, if you saw a rose,
  Plucked quick in June's surrender,
You'd wish it back upon the bough,
  To wither in November.

I wonder, if you watched the moon,
  The tempest's rack outstripping,
You'd grieve to see its silver prow
  In cloudless ether dipping.

I wonder, if you heard a thrush
  Laugh out amid the clover,
You'd weep because its cage door oped—
  Its captive days were over.

I wonder, if, some happy day,
  When you have found your haven,
You'll mourn to find this one dear friend
  Had been so long in heaven.

When I die bury me by the sea. Let my first hundred years in the spirit be spent on a sunny sand-bank watching the sapphire tides break over a bluff of lifted rocks. What is any earthly trouble but a dissolving dream, when one may bury the face in golden moss and sniff the salt spume of the sea! Over the blue verge of the horizon lies Spain, and I build its castles hourly here in my heart. A distant echo rings in my ears of trucks driven over stony streets, of the crack of the cabman's whip and the shout of profane teamsters, but the only semblance to cruel driver and jaded beast of burden seen in the seaside paradise of which I write is a fat huckster and a still fatter donkey who draws the large man where he (the donkey) listeth. Here on this lifted moorland, if one wishes to go anywhere he rises up and goes forth on a carpet of crimson moss and yellow grass and is driven by a chariot of untired winds. Behind us are miles of purple moss swept by ragged shreds of September fog, and musical, here and there, with bells of grazing herds; while before us, behind us, and all around us stretches the boundless, unfathomable and mysterious sea.

Did you ever hear of the island of Avilion? That enchanted place where "falls not hail, or rain, nor ever wind blows loudly," whose orchard lands and bowery hollows lie lapsed in summer seas? I found it one day when I was sailing on Casco bay in a boat hardly bigger than a peanut shell. Tennyson found it long ago in a dream, and to it he sent the good King Arthur that he might "heal him of his grievous wound" within the balm of its heavenly peace. But I found it in reality, and to it I took a careworn lady and a work-weary brain, that I might perchance renew under its sunny spell a strength that was well-nigh spent. I found my island under another name, to be sure, but I rechristened it within the first hour of my landing. It is not the place, my dear, for featherheads and butterflies, this island of Avilion. It is not the place for the descendants of Flora McFlimsy to go with their new gowns and their French heels. All such would vote my little island a bore, and run up a flag for the first inland-bound steamer to put into port and carry them away. It has no ball-room, no promenade-hall under cover, no brass band, no merry-go-round, but instead it has meadow-lands that are brimful of bird songs; it has wild strawberries that bring their ruby wine to the very lips of the laughing sea; it has such sunsets as visit the dreams of poets and the skies of Italy; it has great rocks that are woven all over with webs of wild convolvulus vine, whose airy goblets of pink and blue hold nectar for the booming bee to sip; and it has marguerite daisies by the tens of thousands, and wild roses that carry the tint of your baby's palm and the honey of sugar-sweet dew within the inclosure of their small curled cup. It is hardly bigger than a Cunarder, this little Chebeague island, whose name I changed to Avilion, and from wave-washed keel to flowery bowsprit the eye never lights upon a defilement or a stain. It is the only place in all my wanderings where I never found a peanut shell nor a tin can thrown out to defile nature's beauty.

There was not a single bad odor on my island during the whole ten days of my tarrying, and I am told by those who are old inhabitants that such a thing never was known to it. A soft wind is always blowing, but the only merchandise it carries is wild thyme perfume and the fragrant airs that waft from meadow-lands and old-fashioned gardens full of spice pinks and cinnamon roses. Now and then a hunter's fog slips the leash of its viewless hounds and with noiseless "halloo" scours the island for the prey it tracks but seems never to corral. Now and then a sudden tumult seizes the tides that climb and fall on the shiny rocks and the air is full of the throb of soft drums and the music of flutes that are beat and blown a moment, then die away as quickly as they came, like a strolling band that marches through a village street, then over the hills and far away. Now and then a troop of crows rise silently from out the shadow of the pines and go sailing between the lazy eyes that follow and the sun, until, settling down upon some meadow stacked with new-cut hay, they break into clamorous laughter that taunts you with its shrill derision. Always, from dawn to dewfall, the world about little Chebeague is full of swallows that dart and soar and flit like shadows.

They seldom sing, and yet the few notes they thread upon the air sparkle like diamonds where they fall. Some strange bird, with a low, sleepy song like the crooning of a child that is half asleep, or like a shepherd boy's pipe idly blown beneath the noonday willows, is always haunting the groves of Avilion with an undiscovered presence. I have spent hours looking for him, yet never found him. Sometimes I have been led to half believe the fellow exists only in the fancy of a spellbound idler like you and me.

Just at sunset a little feathered violinist of the island whips out his fiddle and draws the bow so delicately across its vibrant strings, while the golden sun slips tranquilly beneath the tinted waters of Casco bay, that the soul of the listener is fairly attenuated like a high C diminuendo with the spell of so much beauty. I don't know the name of the bird either, but he is going to sing for us all in heaven later on. Such performers do not end all here any more than Beethoven did.

It was my custom during the time I spent at Little Chebeague to devote the entire day to strolling or lying at length upon the rocks—

Nothing but me 'twixt earth and sky;
An emerald and an amethyst stone,
Hung and hollowed for me alone.

I grew to love the solitude with all my heart, and the thought of returning to the mainland with its jargon and its bustle was like the thought of tophet to the poor little peri for whom the gate of paradise had swung. Sometimes I would board the small boat that two or three times a day threads in and out of the blue water-way and visit adjacent islands hardly less beautiful than my chosen home.

There is Long Island, far more beautiful by reason of its East End, where as yet the tide of a full-fledged summer resort has not come. There is an old-fashioned country roadhouse, such as we knew before the landscape gardener and the boulevard fiend were turned loose upon our rural towns. To follow their windings is heaven enough for me. A fringe of buttercups to fence the way, thickets of underbrush to darken the near distance, constant little ups and downs where the road slips into hollow to follow the call of a romping brook or climb a hill to watch for the sea. Wintergreen berries and russet patches everywhere, and the snow of blackberry bushes in bloom far as the eye can travel.

"There is an old-time rail fence!" cried a visitor from the booming west one day; "my God, let me get out and touch it! I haven't seen anything but barbed wire since I left New England!" And he did get out of the buckboard in which he was driving and chipped away a big brown fence sliver as a memento. These roads I am talking about lead nowhere in particular. They, as often as not, end in a fisherman's back dooryard, but they are sweet as a young girl's caprice while they last.

One day we strolled across one of the islands and found a battlement of rocks on the seaside that it would have taken a solid month to explore. Oh, there was enough on the bar at ebb tide at Avilion to while away an age of idle time.

Sometimes we took it into our heads to ride. Then the choice lay between Charlie the Christian—so named for his good behavior and gentle ways—and the one roadster the island produced, a nag in the rough, who held his head high and cavorted with the stride of a jamboreeing boy.

The choice made, the hour must be

watched to catch the low tide over to Big Chebeague, for there are no wagon roads in Avilion. Six hours of safety, as to the low water mark, is the limit of one day's riding, and much can be done in the way of riding in a half-dozen hours' time. A spin across the bar, the climbing of a rocky road, a sweep of seaward-facing pike, with dips into ferny hollows and ascents to pine-crowned bluffs, make the trip worth recording, and if to the exhilaration of the ride you add a dismount now and then to gather wintergreen and pick roses, with a loiter through a churchyard where many Hamiltons, both pre-Adamite and ante-historic, are sleeping the sleep of the just, you have the whole meaning of an afternoon outing on Big Chebeague.

Every evening after supper there was a pilgrimage to the west side of the island, not to be dispensed with by descendants of those remnant tribes that once worshiped the sun. Ranging from north to south as far as the eye can sweep, from westward, fronting little Chebeague, lies Casco bay, the loveliest bit of water in all the world. I say unhesitatingly the loveliest, because I do not believe that Naples, nor Sorrento, nor any far-famed Italian watering-place can match the coast of Maine for beauty. Into this bay, like petals from a wind-shaken blossom tree, are dropped hundreds of islands. Far to the west the White mountains melt upon the horizon in airy outline of blue, and over all each day is repeated the ancient miracle of the sun's decline. Sometimes a single cloud, like a tomb, receives the bright embodiment of day and hides it from our sight behind such draperies as orient never wrought nor monarch dreamed. Sometimes this fair god lies at length upon a bier of purple porphyry, while flakes of crushed gems strew his couch with rainbow dust, and all the air is full of rose-red censers, edged with gold. Sometimes he drops below the verge, holding to the last a wine cup brimmed with sparkling vintage that spills and trickles down the hills. Sometimes he returns in an afterglow, as the dead come back to us in dreams, the tenderer and the sweeter for their second coming. However the sun may set in Avilion, each setting is the most beautiful and best to be desired.

I heard someone bewailing the death of a friend the other day. The staff on which he had leaned, the bread which had ministered to his needs, the very light that had filled his eyes seemed caught away, and he mourned as one for whom there was no comfort possible. I saw a mother leaning above an empty crib, whose dainty pillow no nestling head should ever press again. I marked the terrible yet voiceless grief that ate at a bereaved father's self-control, until no windblown reed was ever so shorn of self-reliant strength. I saw a wife whose love had sunk within the grave where her young husband was laid, as the sun sets within a cloud of stormy night. I saw an old man bow his snowy head because the faithful one whose hand had lain in his for more than fifty years had vanished from his sight forever. I heard a little child lamenting at bed-time the lullaby song which its dead mother's tender lips should never sing again. But sadder than all these things, more tragical than any death which merely picks the blossom of life and bears it onward to heaven, as the gardener plucks the choicest rose to grace some festival of joy, is the scene when a trusted friendship dies; when faith which has endured the test of years gives up the breath of loyal life and sinks to hopeless unawakened death. Never think that you have shed your bitterest tears until you have stood at such a death-bed. Think not the measurement of any mortal grief has been found until you have sunk the plummet-line of such a sorrow. That grave shall never burst its sheath to let the soul of friendship's betrayal free, like a lily on the Easter air. That door shall never swing like the bars of a cage to let a murdered faith flash forth like the plume of a singing bird to seek the stars. Over the grave of a dead and buried trust no resurrection-note can ever sound like a bugle-call across the dewy hills to rouse the sleeper from his couch. God pity all who linger by the heaped-up mound where love's forgotten dreams lie buried, and grant oblivion as the only surcease for their bitter sorrow.

The days and nights swing equally upon the golden balance of time. The year is whitening with its crop of frost-blossoms from which no harvest-home has ever yet been called. Like an unwritten page, the new year lies before us in untrodden fields of shining snow. God grant the footsteps of Death be not the first to track the unbroken path that lies before us. May joy and peace and love, like the roots of the violets under the snow, quicken and blossom for all of us as the year advances, and may our progress be, like January's, right steadily onward unto June!

As I write there is a sudden break in the hush of night, and faint and clear and sweet upon the listening ear falls the sound of "taps" from the camp in Fort Sheridan woods. I drop my pencil and listen to it, as I always do, with almost a spirit of reverent awe. The hard day's work is done, the time for rest has come, and over all the busy camp silence falls like the shadow of a brooding wing. The new moon, half hidden by drifting clouds sends a rippling play of silver through the woodbine leaves, and from the top of the maple tree, a thrush dreams forth a bar of liquid music in its sleep. All the world is going to sleep, and

Rosemary and Rue.

God grant, say I, that when the time for the final good-night has come for you and for me the call for "taps," blown from some celestial bugle the other side the mystic gate may fall as sweetly upon our ears and find us as ready to sink to slumber.

Did you ever hunt for eggs in a haymow? If you did you can remember just how, with bated breath, you crept through the fragrant glooms of the old barn and searched the dusty place for nests. You can recall, perhaps, the shaft of sunlight that broke through the crevice of the door and showed you old speckle-top in her corner. You can hear again her furious cackle when you dislodged her from her nest and gathered the warm eggs she had hovered under her wings. You remember the excitement of the search and the perfection of content which settled within your soul as you gathered the basketful of milk-white eggs upon your arm and picked your way down the steep ladder which led to the main floor and "all out doors." Scarcely any excitement or exhilaration of later years can compare with the joy of hen's-nest hunting when you were young.

Did you ever go berrying? With a tin pail swinging from your wrist and your oldest gown upon your back, have you climbed the hill, jumped the fences and sought the side-hill pasture where the blackberries grew purple in the shade? Can you recall much, in all the years that thread between that happy time and this, which can transcend the pleasure of those wildwood tramps? Even now I seem to fix my eyes upon a clump of bushes by the old rail fence. They are domed high with verdure and show dusky hollows underneath, where, my skilled eye tells me, lurk spoils fit for Bacchus and all his nymphs. I part the leaves, a snowy moth flutters out of the green dusk and wavers like a snowflake in the warm, sweet air. I carefully reach my hand away inside the fairy bower of crumpled leaf and twisted vine and draw it forth purple with the juice of overripe berries that dissolve at a touch. With these I fill my pail, and all too often, I blush to own it, my mouth also, until twilight sends me home saturated with sunshine, late clover blooms and berry juice.

Ah, my dear, all this was fun while it lasted, but there is a more exciting quest than hunting eggs or finding berries, in which we all of us engage as the years of our mortal pilgrimage go hurrying by. It is the search for happiness—a search we never give up nor grow too old to maintain. Forgetting the disappointments and the satieties of the dead years, we look forward to the new as the hidden nestfull of unchipped shells of fresh experience and untried delights. God bless us all, and prosper us to find the eggs and the berries before we die. Perhaps the service of love we do others shall prove the bush that bears the sweetest and the ripest clusters, and the nestfull that shall develop the whitest store of all life's opportunities.

A genuine mother could no more raise a bad boy into a bad man than a robin could raise a hawk. When I say "genuine mother," I mean something more than a mother who prays with her boy, and teaches him Bible texts, and sends him to Sunday-school. All those things are good and indispensable as

far as they go, but there is a lot more to do
to train a boy besides praying with him,
just as there are things necessary to the cultivation of a garden besides reading a man-
ual. To succeed with roses and corn one
must prune, weed and hoe a great deal. To
make a boy into a pure man, a mother must
do more than pray. She must live with him
in the sense of comrade and closest friend.
She must stand by him in time of temptation as the pilot sticks to the wheel when
rapids are ahead. She must never desert
him to go off to superintend outside duties
any more than the engineer deserts his post
and goes into the baggage car to read up
on engineering, when his train is pounding
across the country at forty miles an hour.

A LITTLE GOLDENHEAD.

Gay little Goldenhead lived within a town
Full of busy bobolinks, flitting up and down,
Pretty neighbor buttercups, cosy auntie clovers,
And shy groups of daisies, all whispering like
    lovers.

A town that was builded on the borders of a
    stream,

By the loving hands of nature when she woke
 from winter's dream;
Sunbeams for the workingmen taking turns with
 showers,
Rearing fairy houses of fairy grass and flowers.

Crowds of talking bumblebees, rushing up and
 down,
Wily little brokers of this busy little town,
Bearing bags of gold dust, always in a hurry,
Fussy bits of gentlemen, full of fret and flurry.

Gay little Goldenhead fair and fairer grew,
Fed on flecks of sunshine, and sips of balmy dew,
Swinging on her slender foot all the happy day,
Chattering with bobolinks, gossips of the May.

Underneath her lattice on starry summer eves,
By and by a lover came, with his harp of leaves;
Wooed and won the maiden, tender, sweet and
 shy,
For a little cloud home he was building in the
 sky.

And one breezy morning, on a steed of might,
He bore his little Goldenhead out of mortal
 sight;
But still her gentle spirit, a puff of airy down,
Wanders through the mazes of that busy little
 town.

Where shall we go to find the fit symbol of Easter? To the encyclopedia that we may post ourselves as to word derivations and root meanings? As well send a child to a botanist to find the meaning of a rose! To fitly understand the true significance of Easter time, find some slope in early April that the sun has found a few short days before you. Lay your ear close to the ground that you may hear the fine, soft stir within the bosom of the warm earth. Note how the mold is filling with its new birth of flowers. There is not a covert in all the awakening woods that has not a little nestling head hidden behind the dead leaves. The breath of a sleeping child is not more peaceful than the sway of the wind flower upon its downy stem. The flush on a baby's cheek is not more delicate than the tint of each gossamer petal. To what shall we liken the grass blades already springing up along the loosened water ways? To fairy bowmen, led by Robin Hood's ghost through winding ways from forest on to the sparkling sea. To what shall we liken the violet buds spread thick beneath the country children's feet? To constant thoughts of God that bloom even in the grave's dark dust. To what shall we liken the twinkling leaves that shine in the dim depths of the woods? To lights at sea, that tell some fleet is sailing into port. To what shall we liken the shy unfolding of the lilac buds? To the poise of a slender maiden who leans from out her lattice to hearken to a lover's song. To what shall we liken the cowslip's valiant gold? To the shining of a contented spirit with a humble home. To what shall we liken the brooding sky and the warmth of the all-loving sun? To the potency of a gentle nature intent on doing good, and the yearning of a tender heart to bless and save. Is there a nook so dark and forbidding that the beautiful Easter sunshine cannot enter and woo forth a flower? Is there a rock so impervious that the April wind may not find lodgment for a seed in some crevice, and there uplift a bannered blossom? Is there a cold, resentful bank wherein the late snow lingers that shall not finally cast off its disdainful ice and flash into verdure in response to the patient shining of the sun? Is there a grave in all the land so new and desolate that Easter time cannot find a violet among its clods and paint a rainbow within the tears that rain above it? To nature's lovers, then, as to the truly

Christian heart, the significance of Easter is found in the reviving garden and in the awakening woods. It means resurrection after death, blossom time after the bareness of woe, the cuckoo's cry after the silence of songless days, and the smile of a pitying All-Father after the orphan time of the soul's bereavement and seeming desertion.

Another blessed thought to be gained in the contemplation of nature's sure awakening from the long lethargy of her winter's sleep is that, however fearful we may be that death's reign shall be eternal, as constant as day dawn after midnight, or shining after storm, shall be the Easter of the soul. We do not need to pray for April; it comes. Nor do we need to pray for release from the first dark dominion of fear and dread when our beloved are snatched from our arms. Such experience is only the transient reign of winter in the heart, while yet the soft wing of April stirs upon the horizon's misty verge and the promise of violets is in the lingering darkness of the air. Remember this: The same power that sends us November is planning an April to follow, and out of the snowfall evolves the whiteness of the annunciation lily.

It has always seemed to me that, beautiful as Christ's birthday ought to be and full of tender significance as we may make the hallowed Christmas time, a deeper tenderness attaches to these Easter days. The Sinless One had lived out the span of his mortal years; he had suffered and been betrayed; had struggled through Gethsemane, up to the thorn-crowned heights of Calvary, and yet, through all, carried the whiteness of a saintly soul, to cast its dying petals, like a white rose, wind-shaken yet yielding perfume even in death, in the utterance of that prayer for universal forgiveness, the most wonderful that ever ascended from earth to heaven—"Father, forgive them, for they know not what they do!" The song that ushered in the birthtime of those sanctified years was an invocation of peace and good will, beneath which the morning stars were shaken like banners before the oncoming of a glorious prince, but the prayer that ascended from Calvary was the plea of a betrayed and anguished soul for universal charity and forgiveness from God to man. Let us rejoice, then, when Christmas days bring gladness to our hearts and homes, but let us forgive and bless when Easter lays its stainless lily at our feet. There is constant need for charity and forgiveness in a world so full of self-blinded and ignorant evil-doers. They do not always know what they do, these rude and riotous betrayers of Christ; and all the more need, then, for compassion, and that divine pity that, even from the cross, could invoke heaven's pardoning love.

If you have a friend who has wronged you, forgive him to-day, for Christ's sweet sake. If you have a boy who has gone astray, reach out your arm and win him back, while yet the Easter violets glow upon the chancel rail. If you have a daughter who has been undutiful, take her in your arms and ask God to forgive you both— you for your lack of sympathy, as well as her for her waywardness. So shall you understand the meaning of Easter, the resurrection time of love, the fulfillment of its promise from out the icy negation of the grave.

A few thoughts about death before we turn to other symbolizations of the season. It is all a mistake, it seems to me, to make death a menace and a dread in the minds of the young. Does the farmer go forth with tears to plant the seed for the coming harvest? Does the scientist mourn above the chrysalis that lets a rare butterfly go free? Does the navigator rebel when a bark that has been tempest-tossed and storm-driven enters port? Teach the children that death is all that makes life endurable; that it is the sheaf of ripened wheat, or the budding flower, plucked from the earth's dark mold; that it is the flight of the bird, the home stretch of the yacht. We love each other, but what is it that makes human love any nobler than the chirruping of birds if not its duration? And it is only death that makes our loves immortal. Time enthrals them with fear and environs them with alarms; death lifts them into the region of eternal joy. Take away the reality of our faith in the life to come and Easter would mean no more to us than it means to the browsing cattle that munch the violet buds and trample the bright promises of the year under foot. The comforting view of it all is, that here we are only learning to love. We are like birds that sit upon the edge of the nest, and flutter, and chirp, and dread to fly away. What shall the bough whereon our nest was rocked with many a storm be when we have learned to spread these tiresome wings and rejoice in the blue space of the boundless air? The heroism of love, the faithfulness of love, the grandeur, patience and magnificence of love shall only be revealed when the soul has left the shadows and spread its wing in the empyrean of heaven's blue.

There is a small boy who lives at our house with whom I wage an unending warfare on the subject of clean hands. The sun never goes down nor yet arises upon a harmonious adjustment of the mooted question. There are more tears shed, more dire threats made, more promises broken, more anguish endured on that one account than upon any other under the sun.

The boy dwells under a ban as somber as the seven-fold curse of Rome. His sisters nag him, his grandmother prays for him, his mother pleads with him, his girl friends flout him, but in spite of all he continues to wear his hands in half tints. But the other evening he made an announcement that caused even the young person to remark:

"Well, I'd rather see you with your soiled hands than see you such a dude as that!"

"Gee!" said the boy, "but some of the kids that go to our school are queer ducks!"

"Don't use so much slang," cried his mother; "why can't you call a boy a boy as well as a 'kid' and a 'duck;' and whatever do you mean by 'Gee?'"

"They bring little cushions to school," continued the boy with only a swift hug in answer to his mother's question, "and they put 'em under their hands when they play marbles, so's they won't get their hands dirty. Gee whiz, but I'm glad I ain't such a fool!"

And in spite of her desire to see him a bit more solicitous as to personal elegance his mother could but echo the boy's self-congratulatory remark.

What on earth is going to become of us if this awful wave of effeminacy which has struck the race does not soon subside? Earmuffs and galoshes, heated street cars in April and double windows up to rose time have done their best to make molly coddles out of men, but when we are starting a generation of boys to play marbles with cushions to rest their hands on the sex had better abolish hats and trousers and take to hoods and shoulder shawls. Give me a boy and not a pocket edition of an old woman. He need not be a tough nor a bully, nor need he be cruel nor untender because he is a boy, but I want him jolly and brave and up to every harmless prank that's going. I want him to use slang and wear muddy shoes, slam doors and make all sorts of futile feints at keeping his hands clean, provided, always, he appreciates the opportunity offered to show the gentleman that's in him by never appearing at table looking like a tramp. Even that is better, though, than being a "sissy." Give him time and the untidiest boy in the world will develop into a gentleman, but eternity itself could not evolve a man out of a boy who plays marbles with a cushion!

As I was walking down Dearborn street the other day, close upon the gloaming, I chanced to meet two pretty girls, not the only two in this big city, perhaps, but two of the fairest. One had hair like the tassel of ripe corn when the sunshine finds it; the other's head was crowned with dusky braids, and the eyes of the two were brimful of laughter as a goblet new-filled with wine. Surely such pretty girls should carry queenly hearts, thought I, and with my old trick of catching topics in the air, I loitered a little on my way to hear what such fair lips might be saying. Said one: "I really don't care to marry him; he is such a darned fool! but he will give me everything I want, and I suppose I shall." I stayed to hear no more. If I had caught a yellow-bird swearing, or seen the first robin appear in Joliet stripes, the revulsion from pleasure to disgust could not have been more sudden. Is this all the lesson the world has taught you, my pretty maiden? To soil your lips with slang and sell yourself for fine clothes and the chance of unlimited display! Forecasting the life of such a girl is like forecasting an April day that dawns in tints of purple and gold, and ends in tempest and the blackness of night. Beauty is a glorious heritage, indeed, but to see it worn by such types as you, my pretty dears, is like seeing a queen's crown on the head of a parrot, or a royal scepter in the grasp of a monkey.

Rosemary and Rue.

Niagara Falls! What heart is so stolid, what appreciative spirit so calloused over with the hard crust of stoicism not to rise and shout before the wonder of its magnificence? When a man or woman gets so blase as to thrill no more over Niagara Falls, let them be salted down with last year's hams and hung on a hook in the quiet seclusion of a smokehouse.

First we took our way over the bridge that leads to the beautifully kept Goat Island and, alighting from the carriage, stood for a time with the full splendor of the American fall in our faces. A fascination that could not be shaken off held the eyes upon that never-stayed torrent of sun-illumined jewels. Diamonds they were, and great uncut emeralds, with here and there a rain of fiery rubies, that tumbled from off the lifted ledge of imperishable rock. And where the volume widened, until it became an avalanche of snowy foam, shot through and through with needles of light, it seemed to us that the law of gravitation had been forever abandoned, and falling tons of water, losing kinship drop with drop, were floated skyward again to find a home in heaven. Down-shooting rockets of silver foam unfallen, yet always in the air! Canopies of cloud, dissolving into fine dust-like roadside pollen! Draperies of spray unrolled in noiseless splendor from the blue background of an endless day! Explosions in mid air of thunderous torrents that turned to carded wool on the way from heaven to earth! While I stood and watched it all somebody profaned the air with a vulgar word, and I looked for a flaming sword from the omnipotent hand to smite him where he stood. To swear, or even to think an unholy thought in such a holy of holies, deserves the penalty of death as much as did the desecration of the temple in ancient times.

Shifting our place from point to point, we found ourselves at last standing on the very verge of the Horseshoe falls, where, crowned with living green, it slips over the crumbling ledge and loses itself in a dazzling whirl of spray. Although I have stood in that same spot many times I am proud to remark that I have never stood there yet without saying my prayers. The sight is too much for the puny ego that animates this little capricious whiff of dust we call our mortal body, and now, if never before, the soul that retains one particle of the divine within it turns to God as the sunflower follows the sun. While we stood entranced by the sublime beauty of the scene a mighty wind arose suddenly and great clouds were called across the sky to the sending of a swift alarm. Before the breath of the wind the mists were tumbled far and wide like feathers, and a rainbow that arched the whole was demolished into nothingness only to be kindled again as a flame in the whimsical breath of the riotous air. One moment the atmosphere was a fairy flower garden, full of violets, roses, green feathery ferns and passion-tinted tulips brimming over with gold. The next some giant hand reached forth and plucked and bore each flower away. A suffusion of color followed every flood of sunshine, as a pomegranate runs with juice at the touch of a knife, only to be succeeded by pale wafts of colorless, interminable spray, where a cloud caught the too eager sun within its soft eclipse.

If the Lord left any snakes in Paradise after the settlement of the primal fuss they took the shape of the man who is a confirmed cynic and pessimist. The man who has no faith, no enthusiasm, no candor, no sentiment. The man who laughs at the mention of good in the world, or virtue in women, or honor among men. The man who calls his wife a fool because she teaches his little children to say their prayers, and curls his lip at any belief in the world beyond the grave. The man who never saw anything worth admiring in the sky when the dawn touches it, or the stars illumine it, or the clouds sweep it, or the rain folds it in gray mists of silence. The man who lives in this sparkling, shining world as a frog lives in a pond or a toad in a cellar, only to croak and spit venom. The man who never saw anything in a rose aglint in the sunlight or in a lily asleep in the moonlight, but a species of useless vegetable, the inferior of the cabbage and the onion. The world is overfull of such men, and if I had the right sort of broom I'd sweep them away as the new girl sweeps spiders.

Once I was sailing in a yacht close to the rock-bound coast of Maine.

It was presumably a pleasure cruise, but if ever a poor wretch in purgatory had a harder time of it I am sorry for him.

The fog was thick, the ground swell was enough to unsettle the seven hills of Rome, and something was wrong with the boat's machinery, so that for hours we lay in the trough of the sea, making no headway and fearful that each moment would be our last. Added to all this there came at short intervals a demoniac blast from a fog horn which rent the air with the clamor of a thousand tongues.

"Look out!" it seemed to shriek over and over again. "Look out, poor fragile wisps of gossamer! The hour strikes for your destruction. Another wave, a little higher than the last, shall suck you down like a shred of foam into the blackness of the sea's dark vortex. Brace up and meet your doom. Look out! Look out! Look out!"

I listened to that fog horn for hours, until the soul within me lay like a spent bird weary with futile beating of useless wings, and I came within a hair's breadth of madness. In fact, I think I had commenced to rave a bit when a brisk wind sprang up that blew the fog away, the crew succeeded in righting the craft and onward we flew out of sound of the terrible fog horn forever.

There are many things in life that remind me of fog horns; there are many occasions that beat upon the soul with just such vociferous clamor.

There are those old-fashioned Bible texts, shouting "hell fire" and "eternal damnation." What are they but fog horns warning us from off a mist-enveloped shore? We cannot shut our ears to them while we lie a furlong off the rocks and listen to their woeful reiteration. Perhaps some chance wind may blow us out to sea, there to escape for the present the unwelcome climax; but we know that underneath the shrouded stars and through the hush of midnight forever and forevermore sounds the crash of that brazen alarm. We may not heed it, but the fog horn is there, forget and disown it though we may.

Then there are our birthdays after we grow old enough to understand their significance; what are they but fog horns that sound at intervals to denote that we are drawing near to the final doom of all mankind?

"Sport on," they seem to say, "a little longer; weave your garlands and blow your pretty bubbles while you may, for to-morrow you shall surely die!"

Each year the fog horn blows a louder blast, until finally the softened haze of creeping years, like a white fog in the sea air, muffles the sound, and we sink to rest at last, some of us with the wild clamor hushed to the measure of a good-night song.

Then the holidays. Thanksgivings and Christmases with independence days, like wine-red roses dropped between, what are they but fog horns on the invisible shores of memory? How they mock us with the recollection of vanished joys, and warn us of barren years yet to be.

Gone forever are the dear ones who made gala times and festival happenings bright, and still we linger like boats in the trough of a sullen sea, our motive power wrecked, our sails rent, and listen, listen, listen to the warning that sounds from far off the hazy shore.

"Gone, forever gone," the fog horn cries; "gone down into the sea, the boats that kept you company when the bright-winged fleet put out from port! Lost forever, in storms it seems scarce worth the while to have weathered, since here you toss, alone at last, like driftwood on the chilly tide, and listen forever to the mournful warning of my voice from off the sandbars, warning you that not even love can withstand the beat of time's relentless years."

Our desks are full of miniature fog horns in the shape of unanswered letters.

Our closets hang full of fog horns of varying fabrics. They warn us of the folly of trusting to bargain sales of shoddy goods; they warn us against extravagant tastes when times are hard; they warn us against the lazy mood that neglects the stitch in time that saveth nine.

Every time we are ill the occasion is a fog horn.

Either we have disregarded some law of health and are in the trough of the sea in consequence, or we are flying on to the breakers with ears dulled to the fog horn's din.

We speak with cruel harshness to the old mother who loves us, or to the little child who trusts us. We are sorry for it afterward, and that sorrow is the fog horn that warns us to keep off the reef of temper.

"To-day may be the last day for the mother you have pained or the child you have wronged," it seems to say; "the bed they lie down upon to-night may be the bed of death. See to it, then, that you make each day of life, if possible, the last day of love's opportunity." Did you ever stop to think of what would become the instant concern of all this vast human race if a sudden edict should go forth that only twenty-four hours were left for each man to live? What if an angel should appear to-day at sunset and proclaim in a voice that should reach from world's center to world's rim, "To-morrow at set of sun this globe and all its race of sentient life shall be folded up like a scroll and effaced from heaven's chart!"

What would we all begin to do then, I wonder? I think that everything would be forgotten but love. Envy and hatred, covetousness, jealousy, ambition, selfishness and cruelty would find no place in the hearts of men. We would improve love's latest opportunity to be kind one to another, tenderhearted and merciful. The husband would not be harsh with his wife, nor the wife show waspish temper to her husband, if the last day had come for both. The father would not strike his boy in uncontrolled temper, nor the mother rebuke her careless child, if the knowledge that the end of love's opportunity lay between the uplifted hand and the culprit. We should all be loving and fond and sweet if we only knew. My dear, this very thought, carried out, is but another fog horn. Perhaps death is already near, and the brazen clamor in our hearts which takes shape of an uneasy conscience or of a nameless dread is but the warning in the fog that we are close upon the fatal reef. Ah, the air is full of them! They sound in every waking moment, they mingle with our dreams, they greet our opening eyes, they accompany us when the tired lids fall in slumber. The shore is lined with them and their warning is as ceaseless as the beat of time's receding waves.

But of what use is a fog horn to a vessel that gives no heed? Why uplift them on dangerous reefs if the ship's crew sleeps through their warning and the unconscious captain ignores their hoarse note of alarm?

An unheeded fog horn might as well be silenced, and so, I sometimes think, if we allow our hearts to grow callous to the call that conscience makes, why not be thankful when the warning ceases and silence follows the useless repetition of an unavailing appeal? If I am to be shipwrecked at last I think I would rather run upon the reefs without warning than to drift to destruction to the mocking cadence of an alarm I would not heed. To go down with the sound in my ears of an admonition that might have saved me had I but listened would be the hardest sort of dying.

HER CRADLE.

There are tears on the gentian's eyelids,
    As they lift them, fringed and fair.
Do they mourn for the vanished brightness
    Of my baby's golden hair?

There's a cloud a-droop in the heavens
    That shadows their sunny hue.
Does it dream of the lovelight tender
    In my baby's eyes so blue?

The golden rod pines in the forest,
    The aster pales by the brook.
Do they miss her fairy footfall
    In each dim and flow'ry nook?

> Now, all through this beautiful weather,
>   Wherever I walk, I weep;
> For I think of the desolate cradle
>   Where my baby lies asleep.

The other night, as I was listening to "taps" in a neighboring military camp, a longing came over me for a silver bugle of my own, that I might blow a message to the drowsy world. We all listen to that fellow up at Fort Sheridan, when he gives the command for "lights out!" just because he blows it through a bugle. He might come out and say what he had to say in tones anywhere between a cornet and a clap of thunder, and the effect would be nothing to what it is when the notes filter through a silver mouthpiece. And how exquisitely the last strains of that nightly call linger on the ear! They melt into the starry glooms, and throb through the dim spaces of the woods like golden bubbles or the wavering flight of butterflies. Whenever we hear them we think of Grant, asleep in his grave by the mighty river, of his work well done, and the rest that dropped upon his pain-racked life at last like a soft and rainy shadow on a thirsty land. We think of hosts of brave men who fill soldiers' graves all over this blood-bought heritage of ours. We think of hearts that once beat high, for long years silent as stones to all our cries and tears. We think of a host of things, solemn and hushed, and sacred, and drop to sleep at last with an indistinct purpose in our hearts to so conduct ourselves that when the Death Angel blows "taps" for us, we shall leave a record behind us to be read through fond, regretful tears, and enshrined in golden characters upon the tablets of memory.

Now, if I had a bugle instead of a pen, to work with, and if I could stand out under the stars on a hushed summer night and deliver my message through its silver throat, perhaps the world that reads me might be thrilled into earnest purpose more readily than it is when exhorted from a pencil point or a quill. The first message I should ring through that bugle of mine would be the command, "Don't fret!" However comfortless and forlorn you may be, don't add to your own and the world's misery by fretting. There never yet was a sorrow that could not be lived down; there never yet was one that could be cured by worry.

When the cows get into the corn and the chickens into the flower-beds, the sensible man chases 'em out first, repairs the damage next, and, lastly, fastens up the break in the garden wall by which the marauders got in. What would you think of a farmer who went into his bedroom to pray before he chased out the cows, or of a woman who threw her apron over her head and wept long and loud because the hens were scratching up her pink roots, instead of "shooing" them a half-mile away with a broom? Most troubles come upon us as the cattle and the hens get into the corn and the garden patch, through a broken fence or a carelessly unguarded gate. It is our own fault half the time that we are tormented, and the sooner we repair the damage and mend the fence, the better. Time spent in useless bewailing, in worry and disquietude, is lost time, and while we wait the mischief thickens. Take life's trials one by one, as the handful of heroes met the host at Thermopylae, and you will slay them all; but allow them to marshal themselves on a broad field while you are crying over their coming or praying for deliverance, instead of arming yourselves to meet them, and they will make captives of you and keep you forever in the dungeon of tears. Is your husband too poor to buy you all the fine clothes you want, or to keep a carriage, or to surround you with pleasant society and congenial friends? Very well, that is certainly too bad, but what's the use of being forever in the dumps about it? Get up and help him keep the cows out of the corn, and perhaps you'll have a golden harvest yet. A sullen, discontented wife is a millstone around any man's neck, and he may be thankful when the good Lord delivers him from her. Whatsoever is worth having in this world's gifts is worth working for, and wedlock is like an ox-team at the plow. If the off-ox won't pull with the nigh one, it has no claim with him upon the possible future of a comfortable stall and a full bin. Out upon you, then, Madam Gruntle, if you sulk, and pout and fret your days away because your husband is a poor man and spends most of his time chasing the cattle, calamity and failure out of his wheat patch. He may possibly be one of fortune's numerous ne'er-do-wells, but in that case all the more reason you should not fail him. Bent reeds need careful handling, and smoking flax gentle tending, else they will perish on your hands and disappoint both you and heaven. All the more reason that you should be cheery and strong and ready to do your part, if the man you married, because you dearly loved him (remember!) is unable to do all that he promised. That is, always provided he is weak and unfortunate, rather than desperately wicked. A woman has no call to stand by any man if he is a wretch and shows no desire to be anything else. The Lord himself never helped a sinner until he showed some desire to be saved. Less repining, then, a little more forbearance with one another's shortcomings, and a little more loyalty to the promise "for better or for worse," will ease up much of the burden of dissatisfied and disappointed wedlock.

Another message that I should blow through that bugle, if I had it at my lips to-night, would be: "Be true!" And I should ring it out so long and loud, I think, that the moon would stop to listen, and the sleepy heads in every home in the land would rise from their pillows like nightcapped crocuses out of the snow. For heaven's sake, if you have a principle or a friend, be true to them. Make up your mind, whether or no your principle is solid and has God and justice on its side, and then be true to it right down to death, or, what is harder, through misunderstanding and obloquy. And if you have a friend, such as God sometimes gives a woman or a man, faithful through all betiding, staunch in your defense and tender in your blame, stand true to that friend until the grave's green canopy is spread between you. He may be unpopular and unfortunate, and all the feather-headed crew of society may ignore him, but if you have ever tested his worth as a friend, stand up for him, and stand by him forever. The sun may go down upon his fortunes, and calumny may cloud his name, and you may know in your heart that more than half the world says about him is true, but stand by the man who has once been your true friend. Ingratitude is the blackest crime that preys upon the human soul. The forgetfulness of a favor, or the effacement of a bond sealed with an obligation, is capable only to weak and cowardly natures.

If you have a conviction, and are conscientious in the belief that you are right, be true to your professions. If you are a rebel, be a rebel out and out, and don't be a goat to leap nimbly back and forth over the fence. Never apologize for either your faith or your profession, unless you have reason to be ashamed of it; and, if you are ashamed of it, renounce it and get one that will need no apology.

There are lots of other messages I would like to stand on a hill and blow through a bugle, but the weather is too warm to admit of further effort just now; so we'll postpone the topic for another hearing.

I sat in a fashionable church the other day and listened to a sermon on "The Prodigal Son." How often I have heard the same old story told in the same old way. How familiar I have become with the kind father, the bad son, refreshingly human heir, the veal and the ring! But the last time I heard the story I felt an almost uncontrollable impulse to rise up in meeting and ask the question, "How does the treatment accorded to the prodigal son match the treatment we mete out to the prodigal daughter?"

How far out of our way do we go to accompany his sister on her homeward faring after a season spent among the swine and the husks?

Do we put an 18-karat ring on her poor little soiled finger and place her at the head of our table, even if by good chance she gains an entrance to the home? Do we not more often meet her at the back door when nobody is looking, rush her through the hallway and consign her to the little third story rear room, taking her meals to her ourselves, on the sly, that the neighbors may not find out the dreadful fact that she is at home again?

"Keep yourself very close," we say to her, "and by no manner of means be seen at any of the windows, and you may stay here. You can wear some of your virtuous sister's cast-off clothing, and sleep on the lounge in the nursery, where the servants never think of going since the little folks have grown up, but you must be very penitent, and very humble, and very thankful to God for the mercy you so little deserve."

I think somebody had better write a new parable and call it "The Prodigal Daughter." Perhaps a sermon might be preached from it to touch the unmoved heart.

After all there are two sorts of prodigals—the prodigal who comes home because the cash gives out, and the prodigal who comes because his heart turns back to the old home with such longing as the thirsty feel for water. Neither boy nor girl who comes back for the first-named reason should find a maudlin love awaiting, nor partake of any banquet that the old folks have had to pay for, but the prodigal who returns because there is something left in his or her heart like the music in a shell, which nothing can destroy or hush away to silence, be that prodigal sinful man or erring woman, should find not only the home doors swung wide in welcome, but every doorway in the land wreathed with flowers to bid him enter.

How few people know when to stop. If the preacher knew when to stop preaching, how much more satisfactory the result of his sermon might be. If the genial fellow knew just when to stop telling his good stories, how much keener their relish would be. If the moralizer knew just when to stop moralizing, how much longer the flavor of his philosophy would endure. If the friend knew when to keep still, how grateful his silence would be. If the candid creature who so glibly tells of our foibles knew when to hold his tongue, how much less strong our impulse to slap him would be. If the high-liver knew when to stop eating, how much less sure dyspepsia would be. If the popular guest knew when to withdraw, how much more regretfully we should see him go. If the politician knew when to retire into private life, how much whiter his record would be. If we all knew just when to die, and could opportunely bring the event about, how much truer our epitaphs would be. The court fool who prayed, "Oh God, be merciful to me, a fool!" prayed deeper than he knew, and the man who prays, "Oh God, teach me to know when I have said enough," prays deeper still.

You may talk about California all you will, but match, if you can, the beauty of spring as it comes to us in these northerly latitudes. There is the coy advance and retreat of a woman hard to win; there is the crescendo and diminuendo of heavenly harmonies; there is the dissolving view that glimmers and glows like an opal, or like the mirage of a misty sea. I was in California a year ago, in April time. I found the month that poets love in full splendor, like a queen who never doffs her crown. Violets, roses, lilacs and carnations came all together in a riotous rush. One did not have to woo the season; it was already won. Like a matron crowned with the mid-splendor of her years, the earth received the homage that is due achievement. Nobody caught the sound of the first robin on a rainy morning and heralded it with a shout; the first robin, like the first principle in creation, never existed, for the reason that he was always there. There were no foretellings of green along the watercourses; no prophetic thrills of violets in the air; no uplifting of the hypatica's downy head above the lattice of fuzzy leaves; everything was right where you discovered it, and had been all the year round. Without beginning and without end, spring exists forever, like a picture bound within a book, in the lovely land of the Gringos. But walk out some April morning in the suburbs that surround Chicago. Catch the tonic of the air, like wine ever so delicately chilled with ice. View the lake, like a gentian flower fringed with a horizon fine as silk. Scrape away the leaves and hail the valiant Robin Hood in his suit of green, leading his legion upward to the sun. Without the sound of a footfall or the gleam of a lance, they come to take possession of the earth. Woo the violet to turn her dewy eye upon you, and listen to the minstrel in the tower, where the winds are harping to the new buds. Mark the maple twigs, like silhouettes cut in coral, and the sheath of the wood lily, like a ribbon half unrolled. Rejoice in the flash of the blue bird's wing as it startles the still air, and then say to me, if you dare, that you prefer any other climate to this one that belts the zone of these northern lakes.

Thank the Lord, all ye who can call yourselves healthy. The day has gone by for physically delicate women. This age demands Hebes and young Venuses with ample waists and veritable muscles. Specked fruit and specked people go in the same category in the popular taste. To the question, "How are you to-day?" I for one, always feel like replying in the words of an old Irish servant we once had (God rest her faithful soul wherever it be this windy day!), "First-rate, glory be to God!" It is such a grand thing to be well and strong, to feel that your soul is riding on its way to glory in a chariot, and not in a broken-down old mud-cart. Talk about happiness! Why, a well beggar has a better time of it than a sick king, any day. If, then, like a bird, your strong wing uplifts you above the countless shafts of pain which that grim old sportsman, Death, is ever aiming at poor humanity, count yourself an ingrate if the song of thanksgiving is not always welling from your heart like the constant song of a bobolink singing for very joy above the clover.

What would be thought of a ship that was launched from its docks with flourish of music and flowing wine, built to sail the roughest and deepest sea, yet manned for an unending cruise along shore? Never leaving harbor for dread of storm. Never swinging out of the land-girt bay because over the bar, the waters were deep and rough. You would say of such a ship that its captain was a coward and the company that built it were fools.

And yet these souls of ours were fashioned for bottomless soundings. There is no created thing that draws as deep as the soul of man; our life lies straight across the ocean and not along shore, but we are afraid to venture; we hang upon thte coast and explore shallow lagoons or swing at anchor in idle bays. Some of us strike the keel into riches and cruise about therein, like men-of-war in a narrow river. Some of us are contented all our days to ride at anchor in the becalmed waters of selfish ease. There are guns at every port-hole of the ship we sail, but we use them for pegs to hang clothes upon, or pigeon-holes to stack full of idle hours. We shall never smell powder, although the magazine is stocked with holy wrath wherewith to fight the devil and his deeds. When I see a man strolling along at his ease, while under his very nose some brute is maltreating a horse, or some coward venting his ignoble wrath upon a creature more helpless than he, whether it be a child or a dog, I involuntarily think of a double-decked whaler content to fish for minnows. Their uselessness in the world is more apparent than the uselessness of a Cunarder in a park pond.

What did God give you muscle and girth and brain for, if not to launch you on the high seas? Up and away with you then into the deep soundings where you belong, oh, belittled soul! Find the work to do for which you were fitted and do it, or else run yourself on the first convenient snag and founder.

Some great writer has said that we ought to begin life as at the source of a river, growing deeper every league to the sea, whereas, in fact, thousands enter the river at its mouth, and sail inland, finding less and less water every day, until in old age they lie shrunk and gasping upon dry ground.

But there are more who do not sail at all than there are of those who make the mistake of sailing up stream. There are the women who devote their lives to the petty business of pleasing worthless men. What progress do they make even inland? With sails set and brassy stanchions polished to the similitude of gold, they hover a lifetime chained to a dock and decay of their own uselessness at last, like keels that are mud-slugged. It is not the most profitable thing in the world to please. Suppose it shall please the inmates of a bedlam-house to see you set fire to your clothing and burn to death, or break your bones one by one upon a rack, or otherwise destroy your bodily parts that the poor lunatics might be entertained. Would it pay to be pleasing to such an audience at such a sacrifice? But the destruction of the loveliest body in the world is nothing compared to the demoralization of soul that takes place when women subvert everything lofty and noble within their nature to win the transient regard of a few worthless men of the world. They learn to smoke cigarettes because such men profess to like to see a pretty woman affect the toughness of a rowdy. They drink in public places and barter their honor all too often for handsome clothes in which to make a vain parade, all to please some heathen man, who in reality counts them a great way inferior to the value of a good horse. The right sort of a sweetheart, my dear, never desires to bring a woman down to his own level. He prefers to put her on a pedestal and say his prayers to her. Never think that you are winning an admiration that counts for much if you have to abate one whit of your womanhood to win it. Every time I see a woman drinking in a public resort, making herself conspicuous by loud talk and louder laughter, I think of some fair ship that should be making for the eternal city, with all its snow-white canvas set, rotting at its docks, or cruising, arm's length from a barren land. We were put into this world with a clean way bill for another port than this. Across the ocean of life our way lies, straight to the harbor of the city of gold. We are freighted with a consignment from quarter-deck to keel which is bound to be delivered sooner or later at the great master's wharf. Let us be alert, then, to recognize the seriousness of our own destinies and content ourselves no longer with shallow soundings. Spread the sails, weigh the anchor and point the prow for the country that lies the other side a deep and restless sea. Sooner or later the voyage must be made; let us make it, then, while the timber is stanch and the rudder true. With a resolute will at the wheel, and the great God himself to furnish the chart, our ship shall weather the wildest gale and find entrance at last to the harbor of peace.

When you look at a picture and find it good or bad, as the case may be, whom do you praise or blame—the owner of the picture or the artist who painted it? When you hear a strain of music and are either lifted to heaven or cast into the other place by its harmonies or its discord, whom do you thank or curse for the benefaction or the infliction, whichever it may have proved to be—the man who wrote the score or the music dealer who sold it? You go to a restaurant and order spring chicken which turns out to be the primeval fowl. Who is to blame—the waiter who serves it or the business man of the concern who does the marketing? And so when you encounter the bad boy, whom do you hold responsible for his badness—the boy himself or the mother who trained him? I declare, as I look about me from day to day and see the men and women who play so poor a part in life, it is not the poverty of their performance that astonishes me so much as the fact that it is as good as it is.

I did think I would keep out of the controversy on the low-neck dress question. But there is just one thing I want to say. Did you ever know a sweet young girl yet, one who was rightly trained and modestly brought up, who took to decollete dresses naturally? Is not the first wearing of one a trial, and a special ordeal? It is after the bloom is off the peach that a young woman is willing to show her pretty shoulders and neck to the crowd; and who cares much for a rubbed plum or a brushed peach? I cannot imagine a sweet, wholesome-hearted woman, be she young or old, divesting herself of half her clothes and thrusting herself upon the notice of ribald men. I can sooner imagine a rose tree bearing frog. The conjunction is not possible. The cheek that will blush at the story of repentant shame, that will flame with indignant protest when the skirts of a Magdalene brush too near, yet deepens not its rose at thought of uncovering neck and bust in a crowded theater or public reception is not the cheek of modest and natural womanhood. It is not necessary to be a prude or a skinny old harridan either, to inveigh against the custom. I know full well how contemptible the affectations and hypocrisies of life are. Half that is yielded to evil was meant for good. The high chancellor of Hades has put his seal on much that was originally invoiced for the Lord's own people. But there are some things so palpably shameless that to argue about them is like trying to prove by demonstration that a crow is white. It needs no argument.

THE VETERANS.

Scarce had the bugle note sounded
    For the call of their last defeat;
And still on the lowland meadow
    Lie the prints of their quick retreat.

Above us the bright skies sparkle,
    And around us the same winds blow
That rippled their golden banners
    In that battle so long ago,

When the southwind challenged winter,
    And the rose-ranks routed the snow,
And the hosts of tiny gold coats
    Sprang up from their campfires below,

To charge on the insolent frost king,
  And shatter his lance of ice,
While back to the desolate northland
  They wheeled him about in a trice.

The battle is hardly ended,
  The victory only begun,
Yet I saw the gray-bearded vet'rans.
  To-day, sitting out in the sun.

They nod by wind-rippled rivers,
  They shake in the shade of the oak,
And all the day long they murmur
  And whisper, and gossip, and croak.

And often in wondering rapture,
  They recount the charge they made,
When down from the windy hillsides,
  And up through the dewy glade,

The sheen of their golden bonnets
  Shone out from the green of the leaves,
Like the flight of a glancing swallow,
  Or the flash of a wave on the seas.

They muse in sleepy contentment,
  Or flutter in endless dispute.
For this was a brave cadet. sir,
  And that one a crippled recruit.

Fight over again your battles,
  O veterans, withered and gray;
For a band of northwind chasseurs
  To-morrow shall blow you away.

Once upon a time it came to pass that a woman, being weary with much running to and fro, fell asleep and dreamed a dream.

And in her dream she beheld a mighty host, more than man could number. And of that host, all were women, and spake with varying tongues.

And they bent the body, and sitting on hard benches wailed mightily, so that the air was full of the sound of lamentation, like a garden that wooeth many bees.

And the woman who dreamed, being tender of heart and disposed kindly toward the suffering ones, lifted up her voice saying:

"Why bendest thou the body, oh, daughters of despair, and why art thine eyelids red with tears?

"Yea, why rockest thou like boats that find no anchor, and like poplars which the north wind smiteth?"

And one from among the host greater than man could number made answer, saying:

"Wouldst know who we are, and why we spend our days like a weaver's shuttle that flitteth to and fro in a web of tears?

"Behold we are the faithless and unregenerate handmaids who have served thee, and women like unto thee, bringing desolation unto thy larders, and gray hairs among the braids with which nature hath crowned thee.

"Yea, verily, by reason of our misdemeanors lift we the voice of lamentation in a land that knoweth not comfort."

Now, the woman who dreamed, being full of amazement, replied anon, and these were the words that fell from her lips:

"Sayest thou so? And dwellest thou and thy sisters in Hades by reason of the evil thou hast wrought?"

"Nay, not forever," replied she who had spoken. "We remain but for a season, that our remorse may cleanse our record before we go hence to sit with the blessed ones in glory.

"Not from everlasting unto everlasting is the duration of the penalty we pay for what we have done unto thee, else were there no peace between the stars by reason of our torment and our tears."

And the woman who dreamed beheld many whose fame yet lingered within the shadows of her home.

There was Ann, the fumble-witted, who

piled the backyard high with broken china, yet stayed not her hand when rebuked therefor.

There was Sarah, the high-headed, who refused to clean the paint because she had dwelt long in the tents of such as hired the housecleaning done by other hands, that the labors of the handmaid might be few;

Yea, verily, with such as believed that Sarah and her ilk might have time wherein to be merry rather than toil.

There was Karen, the Swede, who wrapped the bread in her petticoat and refused to be convinced of the error of her ways.

There was Jane, the Erinite, who broke the pump, and Caroline, the Teuton, who combed her locks with the comb of the woman who dreamed.

There was Adaline, the hoosier, who failed to answer the summons of the stranger who knocked at the gates unless she were in full dress and carried a perfumed handkerchief.

There was Louise, who smote the youngest born of the household because he prattled of her dealings with the frequent cousin who called often and sought to deplete the larder.

There was the girl who desired her evenings out and never came home before cock crow.

There was the girl who threw up her place in the family of the woman who dreamed because she was asked to hurry her ways.

There was the girl who wore the hose of her mistress, and took it as an affront when asked to desist.

There was the girl who swore when the chariot of the sometime guest drew nigh, and likewise the girl who refused to remain over night in a dwelling where she was summoned to serve by means of a call bell.

There was the girl who found it too lonesome in the country and left the garments in the washtub that she might hie her to the great city, the social center of which she was the joy and the pride.

There was the girl who was made mad by means of the request that she wash her hands before breakfast.

There was the girl who entertained her callers in the drawing-room while the family was afar off, sojourning in the hills or by the waves of the sea;

Yea, who thought it no evil to bring forth

the flesh-pot and the brandied comfit, that the heart of the district policeman might leap thereat, as the young buck leapeth at sight of the water courses.

There was also the girl who wasted, and the girl who stole; the girl who never tried, and the girl who never cared.

And seeing the multitude the spirit of the woman who dreamed arose within her and she asked of a certain veiled one who seemed to be in charge:

"Tell me, O shrouded one, is there never to be any diminution in the throng that cometh to take their abode in these halls of penitential regret?"

And the spirit in charge made answer, saying:

"No, nor never shall be while fools live and folly thrives.

"It is by reason of the babbling of busybodies that havoc has overtaken the land of thy forefathers.

"There is honor in faithful service, and an uncorruptible crown awaiteth the forehead of her who serveth well.

"It is no disgrace to the comely daughters of men who toil and are put to that they bring in the wherewithal to fill the mouths of the children who call them father—

"It is no disgrace, I say unto you, if such maidens take unto themselves the position of servants in the family of him who prospereth,

"Remembering that one who lived long since and has slept these many years in the tomb of his fathers, spake truly when he uttered these words, albeit framed in rhyme:

"Honor and shame from no condition rise;
  Act well your part, there all the honor lies."

And it came to pass that the woman who dreamed took comfort to herself by reason of her dream.

And she arose from slumber like a strong man who desireth to run a race.

And buckling on more tightly the armor wherein she moved, yea, even with a free hand buttoning the boot and drawing the string, she cogitated unto herself, and these were the words of her cogitation:

"Behold, I will learn a new wisdom that I may be unto my handmaids a friend rather than a taskmistress, that in so doing I may win unto my household the damsel who hath intelligence. And my treatment of her shall be such that many wise ones who call that damsel friend shall decide to do even as she hath done and choose domestic service with a woman who is kind even to the showing of interest in her handmaid's affairs, rather than linger in bondage with the shop girl and her who rattles the tinkling keys of the typewriter machine.

"So doing, my days shall increase mightily in the land, as also the days of her who cometh after me."

Women are either the noblest creation of God or the meanest. A good woman is little less than an angel; a bad woman is considerably more than a devil. And by bad women I do not mean women who drink, or steal, or frequent brothels. The chief weapon of a bad woman is her tongue. With a lie she can do more deadly work than the fellow in the bible did with the jawbone of an ass. Untruth is the fundamental strata of all evil in a bad woman's nature, and with it she is more to be dreaded than many men with revolvers. There is absolutely no protection from a lie. The courts cannot protect from its venom, and to kill a defamer and a falsifier is not yet adjudged as legalized slaughter.

There is one awfully homely woman in Chicago. I met her the other day over in Blank's art gallery. Our acquaintance was brief but sensational. I looked at her, tucked her into my handbag and wept. She didn't seem to mind it, and when, a few hours later, in the seclusion of my chamber, I took her out of the bag and looked at her again, she was more hideous than before.

"You horrible creature!" said I. "If you look like me, better that the uttermost depths of the sea had me."

"But I do look like you," said she, and her voice was weak and low by reason of prolonged exposure to the sun and air, "and Mr. Blank says I will finish up very nicely."

"Do you mean to tell me," I asked, "that my nose is as big as yours?"

"Of course it is," said she; "pictures cannot lie. But comfort yourself with the assurance that a large nose is always an indication of intelligence."

"Intelligence be blessed!" said I, for I was getting excited; "intelligence without beauty is like bread without butter, or a peacock without a tail! If I possess such a nose as yours, madam, I shall take to tract-distributing, galoshes and a cotton umbrella, and forget that I was ever human."

"You talk wildly, as all the rest of them do," said my thin companion. "Listen, for my time on earth is short, I am rapidly fading away, and what I say must be said briefly. If you look about you you will see that there exists, more or less hidden in every breast, the belief of one's own beauty. The mirror, although a faithful friend, can never quite disabuse the mind of that belief, and when the honest camera holds up the actual presentation of one's self as an incontrovertible fact, the disappointment is keen and hard to bear."

"All that may be true," said I, "but not all your assertions can ever make me believe that that dusky mass of hair, brushed back so wildly from those beetling brows, is like my own. You know that mine is soft and brown, and yours looks like the bristles of an enraged stove brush."

"That's the way they all talk," responded the dissolving view, "but you do not stop to consider that under the artist's pencil the shadows will all be toned and softened.

And let me say right here, that that 'beetling brow' is a sign of rare intelligence, much more to be desired than the lower and more——"

"Stop, right there!" I interrupted. "It is not necessary to have a brow like a plate-glass show-window, or like an overhanging cliff, or like a granite paving-stone, to denote intelligence! No, my friend, do not try to lift this shadow from my soul. That mouth that looks like a dark biscuit, that nose that looks like a promontory overhanging an unseen sea, that hair that looks like the ruff of an excited chicken, that brow that looks like a skating-rink, all make me sad. I shall never have my picture taken again. If I look like that it is time I died. In the round of an eventful life I may forget that I even saw you, but until I do I am a tired woman. My mirror may assuage my sorrow, for that either lies or catches me from a different point of view. Vanish then, oh, yellow shade of an unhappy reality. Back to oblivion with you, and heaven grant I never look upon your like again!" So saying, I calmly held the poor but hideous creature in the flame of a gas-jet and smilingly cremated her.

A fairer day than last Sunday was never cradled to rest behind the curtains of night. It began with a flute obligato of sunrise, orbed itself into a full orchestra wherein color took the part of first and second violins, and declined at last into the hush of sunset like the mellow notes of a cello under old Paul Schessling's master touch. Such days visit the earth rarely. They are advance sheets of a story that is going to be told in heaven; preludes to a song that we shall hear in its perfection only when we have got through with the clattering discords of time. Thank God for all such days. They do us more good than we know. The sight of the woods, adorned as only queens are adorned for the court of the king, the sound of falling leaves and lonely bird songs, of hidden lutes, of unseen brooks, tremulous and sweet and low under the russet shadows, uplift our souls and help us to forget, for the time being at least, how tired we are, how worn with the fret of sordid toil and how tormented and misjudged and calumniated we are by those who fain would do us harm. I think if I had time to do some of the things I want to do the first consummation of that happy time would be to build me a little cabin in the woods, where, in utter loneliness, I could forget how full the world is growing to be of folks and how prone they are to do each other harm and hinder rather than help each other on the stony way to heaven.

The other evening, while sitting in the gallery of the Auditorium and looking over the balcony edge at the crowd waiting for the curtain to rise, a strange thought came to my mind. How could hell be more quickly created than by the unmasking of such a crowd as this? Suddenly remove from humanity all power of self-control and conventional dissimulation; force men and women to be natural, and act out every evil impulse latent in their souls, and could Dante himself portray a blacker Inferno? The man whose heart is full of murderous hatred—tear off the mask that hides his perturbed soul, and what a demon would look forth! The woman behind whose amiable seeming lurks malicious envy and snarling temper and crafty deceit—what a pandemonium would ensue when such passion broke forth like straining dogs from the leash! The old man with the saintly face and the crown of hoary hair—could an open cage of foul birds send forth a blacker brood than should fly out from his soul when some omnipotent hand unlatched the bars of its prison and let the unclean thoughts go free? The young man with the perfumed breath and the suave and courtly manner—does any storied hell hold captive blacker demons than the cruel selfishness, the impurities and the secret vices that walk to and fro in his soul like tigers behind their bars? The young girl with face like a rose and the form of a Juno—could anything that hades holds strike greater dismay to the hearts of men than the unmasking of her hidden thoughts? Ah, when the hour strikes for unmasking time in life's parade ball, when death steps forth and with cool, relentless touch unties the knot that holds the silken thing in place that has hidden our true selves from our beautiful seeming, we shall find no more fiery hell awaiting us than that we have carried so long in our hearts.

I would not like to be regarded as a pessimist from the writing of such a paragraph as the above. Sometimes I seek to turn my thoughts upon the crowd and unmask the angel as well as the demon. But I find that the angels, as a general thing, wear no face concealers. They go disguised in poor clothes and scant bravery of attire, but the angel within them is like a singing bird rather than like a silent and chained beast. It reveals itself in songs, like a caged lark. It looks from out the window of the eyes in loving glances and tender smiles; it manifests itself in sweet and cheerful service, like the sunshine that can neither be hidden nor concealed.

Of all the pleasant things to look upon in this fair earth, I sometimes query which is the best, a little child, a fruit orchard in early June, or a young girl. I think the latter carries the day. Did you ever watch a flock of birds sitting for a moment on the mossy gable of a sloping roof? How they flutter and fuss and chirp; how they preen their delicate feathers and get all mixed up with the sunshine and the shadow, until which is bird and which is sunbeam one can scarcely tell. There is a flock of girls with whom I ride every morning, and they make me think of birds and sunbeams. They are so bewitching with their changeful moods and graces that I sit and watch them as one listens to the twitter of swallows. They sweeten up life, these girls, as sugar sweetens dough; they fill it with music as sleigh bells fill a winter night. God bless the girls, the bonnie, sweet and winsome girls, and may womanhood be for them but as the "swell of some sweet time," morning gliding into noon, May merging into June.

There are so many things in this world to be tired of! The poor little persecuted boy in pinafores, sent to school to get him out of the way, doomed to dangle his plump legs all day long from a hard bench, rubbing his grimy knuckles into his sleepy blue eyes and wondering if eternity can last any longer than a public school session, grows no more tired of watching the flies on the ceiling and the shadows on the wall than some folks get of life. Let me mention a few of the things I, for one, am horribly tired of, and see if before my bead is half strung you do not look up from the strand and cry, "Amber, I am with you!"

My dear, I am tired to-day of civilization and all modern improvements. I am tired of the speaking tube within my chamber where the new girl and myself wage daily our battle of the new Babel. She speaks Volapuk, and I do not, consequently she takes my demand for coal as an insult or an encouraging remark, just as the mood may be upon her, and pays no more attention to my request for drinking water than the unweaned child pays to the sighing wind. I am tired of sewer gas and what the scientists call "bacteria" and "germs." I am tired of going about with frescoed tonsils, the result of the three. I am tired of gargling my own throat and the throats of my helpless babes, and the throat of the casual visitor within my gates, with diluted phenic acid to ward off deadly disease. I am tired of nosing drains and buying copperas and hounding the latent plumber that he adjust the water-pipes. I am tired of boiling the cistern

water and waiting for it to cool. I am tired
of skipping from Dan to Beersheba daily for
men to remove the tin-cans, the ashes and
the unsightly rubbish that have emerged
from long retirement underneath the snow.
I am tired of imploring the small boy to
keep his mother's chickens off my porch.
I am tired of digging graves upon the common wherein to bury useless potato-parings,
the unsightly cheese-rind, and the shattered
egg-shell. I am tired of being told that my
neighbor's calf and my neighbor's pet cat,
and my neighbor's blooded stock of poultry
are dying because of the copperas I scatter
broadcast about the mouth of drains. I am
tired of being a martyr to hygiene and a
monomaniac on the subject of sanitary
science. I am tired of sharpening lead pencils. I am tired of speaking pleasantly when
I want to be cross. I am tired of the ceaseless
grind of life, which like the upper and nether
mill-stones, wears the heart to powder and
the spirit to dust. I am tired of being told
that the mark on my left ear is a spot of soil,
and of being implored in thrilling whispers
to wipe it away. I am tired of last year's
seed-pods in spring gardens and of all two-
legged donkeys. I am tired of awaiting a

change in the methods of doing business around at the postoffice, and for the dawn of that blessed day when I shall be permitted to dance upon the grave of the aged being who peddles stamps at the retail window. I am tired of hosts of things besides, but have no time to enumerate them all to-day.

I have tested the rainy weather dress reform. It was pouring when I started from my humble home in the morning, and in spite of the prayers of the Young Person and the sobs of the "Martyr," I arrayed myself in my new, highly sensible and demoniacally ugly suit and weathered the elements. Within two hours it stopped raining; the sun came out and the streets filled with festively attired men and women, and where was I? Stranded on a clear day in garments befitting a castaway! My flannel dress, short skirts and top-boots wasted on fair weather. "In the name of heaven," exclaimed a friend, as I bore down upon him beneath a cloudless sky, "what have you got on?" "Go home! for the love of humanity, go home!" said another. And what was I to do? Await another storm like a crab in its shell, or venture forth and become the by-word of an overwrought populace, the scorn of old men and matrons? Next time I start out in a reform dress I will take along the robes of civilization in a grip-sack.

There is something that is getting to be awfully scarce in this world. Shall I tell you what it is? It is girls. That is what is missing out of the sentient, breathing, living world just now. We have lots of young ladies and lots of society misses, but the sweet, old-fashioned girls of ever so long ago are vanished with the poke bonnets and the cinnamon cookies. Let me enumerate a few of the kinds of girls that are wanted. In the first place we want home girls—girls who are mothers' right hand; girls who can cuddle the little ones next best to mamma, and smooth out the tangles in the domestic skein when things get twisted; girls whom father takes comfort in for something better than beauty, and the big brothers are proud of for something that outranks the ability to dance or shine in society. Next, we want girls of sense—girls who have a standard of their own regardless of conventionalities, and are independent enough to live up to it; girls who simply won't wear a trailing dress on the street to gather up microbes and all sorts of defilement; girls who won't wear a high hat to the theater, or lacerate their feet and endanger their health with high heels and corsets; girls who will wear what is pretty and becoming and snap their fingers at the dictates of fashion when fashion is horrid and silly. And we want good girls—girls who are sweet, right straight out from the heart to the lips; innocent and pure and simple girls with less knowledge of sin and duplicity and evil-doing at twenty than the pert little school girl at ten has all too often; girls who say their prayers and read their Bibles and love God and keep his commandments. (We want these girls "awful bad!") And we want careful girls and prudent girls, who think enough of the generous father who toils to maintain them in comfort, and of the gentle mother who denies herself much that they may have so many pretty things, to count the cost and draw the line between the essentials and the non-essentials; girls who strive to save and not to spend; girls who are unselfish and eager to be a joy and a comfort in the home rather than an expensive and a useless burden. We want girls with hearts—girls who are full of tenderness and sympathy, with tears that flow for other people's ills, and smiles that light outward their own beautiful thoughts. We have lots of clever girls, and brilliant girls, and witty girls. Give us a consignment of jolly girls, warm-hearted and impulsive girls; kind and entertaining to their own folks, and with little desire to shine in the garish world. With a few such girls scattered around life would freshen up for all of us, as the weather does under the spell of summer showers. Speed the day when this sort of girls fill the world once more, overrunning the spaces where God puts them as climbing roses do when they break through the trellis to glimmer and glint above the common highway, a blessing and a boon to all who pass them by.

Is there any flower that grows that can compare with the pansy for color and richness? Others appeal more closely to the heart with fragrance that like a sweet and pure soul more than compensates for lack of exterior beauty, but in all the gorgeous category none rank this velvet flower that lies just now upon my window-sill. There is the purple of Queen Sheba mantled in its soft and shiny texture; the gold of Ophir was not more sumptuous; the light that breaks at dawn across a reef of dove-gray clouds was never more delicate than the violet heart of this lovely blossom. When I want to think of the ideal court of kings, of a royal meeting-place for blameless scions and unsullied princes of the blood, I do not think of old-world palaces and coronation halls—I think rather of a pansy bed in June in full and perfect bloom, a soft wind just bending bright heads crowned with crowns that never yet were pressed on aching brows, and fluttering mantles of more than royal splendor that never yet were wrapped above a corrupt and breaking heart.

MY ROSE AND MY CHILD.

I held in my bosom a beautiful rose,
    All gay with the splendor of June;
Its dew-laden petals like sheen of soft snows,
    Its blush like the sunshine at noon.

But e'en as I held it, I knew it must fade;
   Its bloom was as brief as the hour.
The dews of the evening like soft tears were
      laid
   On the grave of my beauteous flower.

I held in my bosom a beautiful child,
   The splendor of love in her eyes;
No snow on high hills was more undefiled
   Than her soul in its innocent guise.

But I knew that my angel in heaven was missed;
   I knew, like my rose, she must go;
So with heartbreak and anguish her sweet lips
      I kissed—
   She sleeps with my rose in the snow.

It was not so very long ago that I chanced to overhear a lively young woman make this remark about her mother:

"Oh, mamma is nearly always taken for my sister. She never seems like anything more than one of my girl friends."

Poor child, thought I, your state is only another phase of orphanhood, for the young life that has no counsel of motherhood is bereft indeed.

No girlish comradeship, however juvenile and delightful it may be, can possibly take the place of protecting, counseling, mother-love. Not but what the sweetest relationship possible exists where the mother keeps her heart young and in sympathy with her daughter, but there is something else requisite to mother-love.

The best mothers are those who have roomy laps where the big girls love to sit while they whisper the confidences they never could reveal to sister-mothers. They have all-enfolding arms, these right kind of mothers, wherein they gather the tired girl, yes, and the tired boys, too, and rock them to rest and peace, long after their "feet touch the floor."

They used to tell me I must never sit on anybody's lap after my feet reached the carpet, but, thank God, that rule never applied to my mother.

You are never afraid of disturbing mother's "beauty sleep" when you come in late at night if she is of the good reliable sort, as far removed from frisky girl companionship as the moon is from its reflection.

No matter how tardy your home-faring may be she is always up with a lunch and a warm fire in winter or a glass of something cool and fresh in summer to soothe your overexcited nerves, a thing she cannot do if she is forever dancing about with you in your youthful larks. She has a way of calming your tempers with a joke and a caress, of which the sister-mother never dreams. She has also a way of smoothing your hair, which your girl comrade never caught the trick of, for the reason that she is kept too busy curling her own love-locks. When your head aches, the right sort of mother knows just how to pet you to sleep and leave you in a darkened room with a rose on your pillow to greet your waking eyes; if you have a bad cold she knows the cuddly way to coax you to take bitter medicine. She bathes your feet and dries them on nice warm towels. She keeps the younger children from guying you, because your nose is red; in short, she does a thousand nice things of which the sister-mother has no knack whatever.

When great trouble falls to your share, when sharp betrayal pierces your heart, and trusted affection turns to ashes in your hold of what good is the juvenile mother with her girlish tremors and tears? You want somebody next in tenderness to God, to hold you fast and tight. You want somebody who has suffered and grown strong, to soothe your breaking heart. Somebody who can be silent and brave and steady until your fever is passed. The shipwrecked sailor wants a rope rather than a feint of throwing one; the shipwrecked soul wants a heart like rock, rather than a handclasp and a promise. The sister-mother may be all right to go to parties with, but you want something stronger and more steadfast to lean upon in time of perplexity. You want a mother in all the holy significance of the name. However sweet the tie of sisterhood, it cannot be so blessed as the bond of patient, long-suffering, sanctified motherhood.

Seek to keep yourself in sympathy with your girls, then, mothers, but be content to occupy a generation removed from the path they tread. Don't make up in emulation of their beauty; don't seek to win away their beaus and outdress them. Don't go decollete to parties where your girls should be the reigning belles; don't aim to vie with them in fascination or in charm. Be guider and ready counselor, but don't try to be rival. If God has given you a girl child, and that child has grown to womanhood, accept the condition of things and give over being a society belle yourself, abdicating your place for the infinitely sweeter one of mother. You cannot be the right sort of mother and ignore your duty to your child. That duty lies in giving her her rightful place in the line of march from which you are crowded out. Let her carry the banner while you fall back a little. Watch over her, make things easy for her, smooth the little difficulties out of her way, be on hand when she comes home tired and excited to soothe her to rest and calm; counsel her how to pick her way through the snares that are laid for youth and beauty, be a refuge where she can run when the rainy weather sets in, which is sure to fall in the summer time of youth, somewhere and somehow. In short, be just as sympathetic and chummy and sociable as possible, but at the same time make your daughter feel that you are older and stronger and wiser than she, by reason of your motherhood, and that next to God you stand ready to shield her, to guide her, to receive her in time of trouble, to forgive her if she needs forgiveness, and to shrive her if she needs confessing. Teach her that your love can never fail, that your heart is a rock and a fortress and a shield for her to seek in all life's bewilderment, far surer and more steadfast than any other love beneath the stars can ever yield.

When I think of all it means to be a mother I tremble to think how far short of the standard the best of us fall. I would rather have it said of me when I die, "She was a good mother," than that men should get together and exploit my deeds as poet, reformer, artist or story-teller. I would rather feel the dewfall of a child's loving tear upon my face than wear a laureate's crown.

Don't be critical, or censorious, or reserved with your daughters; don't hold them far off and cultivate respect and fear rather than love; don't be self-assertive and cause them to feel their dependence upon you in an unpleasant way; don't be too eager to keep them in the background in little things relating to the home, such as giving them no voice in the arrangement of the room and the domestic regulations. Indeed, I have known more attrition caused in the home circle from this last mentioned point of difference between mother and daughters than almost any other. I know a family, presided over by a good, unselfish woman, who, as a mother, is the most complete failure I ever ran across. Her daughter is of mature age and pronounced opinions, but she is kept in the background and her life rendered most unhappy by the dominant will of the mother whose old-fashioned views as to running the house are directly opposed to more modern customs. The two wrangle continually over the establishment of a dinner hour, the disposal of a light, the drapery of a window, the adjustment of furniture, until there is less harmony under the roof than there is music in a hurdy-gurdy. How much better it would be if that mother would yield a little to the wishes of her daughter; give the latter a chance to display her own taste and carry out her inclination. I don't believe in the mothers and fathers of grown-up daughters always insisting upon the occupancy of the front seats and the leadership of the orchestra.

The mother who can preserve the respect of her children without chilling their love; who can be one with them, and yet apart, in the sense of guiding, aiding and consoling, who can hold their confidence while she maintains the superiority of her wisdom, is the happy and successful mother. The title is a sacred one, made by the chrism of pain and suffering, sanctified by the humanity of Christ and set apart as one of the three of earth's tenderest utterances: "Mother, home and heaven."

Now that the days draw nigh for the return of the birds to our northern woods and dales it is borne in upon me to hold a little "love feast" with the boys. You know what a love feast is, if there was ever a Methodist in your family. It is a good, cozy talk among the brethren and sisters in regard to the best way of putting down the devil, and giving the good angels a chance. And if there was ever need of downing the devil it is in the particular instance of a boy's inhumanity to birds and beasts. I have expressed myself as to horses, and to-day I shall talk about birds. On these spring mornings, when the world is enveloped in a golden halo, from out of which, like angel voices from the quiet depths of heaven, the birds are singing their impromptu of praise, imagine a lot of half-grown men and brutal boys going forth with guns and sling-shots to break up the concert and murder the choristers. I would as soon turn a lot of sharp-shooters into a cathedral at early mass to bring down the surpliced boys and the chanting novices. I tell you, O race of good-for-nothing fathers and mothers, whom God holds directly responsible for the bad boys who desecrate this beautiful world, you are no more fit for the training of immortal souls than a hawk is fitted to teach music to a thrush. You ought to have had a bear-skin and been the trainer of cubs. That your boys develop into brutes and go to state's prison, and perhaps die at the end of a rope eventually, is nobody's fault but your own. If you chance to own a horse or a dog you show some care in its training, but God gives you a boy and you let him run wild. There is no more reason why a boy should be cruel than that a properly-broken colt should kick. The tendency may have been born with him, but good training eliminates it to a great extent, if not entirely. When I was a woman and lived at home, in the happy days before I entered the arena to fight for bread and butter, to say nothing of shoe leather and fuel, I used to gather the village boys about me every spring and try to sow the good seeds of tenderness with one hand, while carefully eliminating the tares with the other. I offered prizes for the best record at the end of the summer. I formed classes, the membership of which pledged themselves, to a boy, to abstain from sling-shots, to cultivate the birds' nests and to withhold their hands from the commission of a single deed of cruelty. Many is the gallon of ice-cream I have paid for to keep those youngsters in the narrow path of rectitude, and many is the time that I have patroled the woods with my boy comrades, keeping watch over the family of a blue-bird or a robin, when the alarm went forth that some unregenerate boy was on the rampage. All the boys whom I could get to join the club I was sure of, for I know the way to a boy's heart, if I can only get the chance at him. For what other purpose did nature turn me out a born cook? And why did she make me a master hand at doughnuts and turnover pies? I have a large and undying faith in the boys, if you will only start them right. The first thing a boy needs is a good mother. He can get along without a father—and I was going to say without a God—for the first few years of his life, but he needs a mother. Not a mere nurse maid to look after his clothes and see that he has plenty to eat at the right intervals, but a good, sweet, companionable mother, with a good, soft breast for him to cry on and two arms to hug him with. He needs a mother who can talk with him and answer his questions, who is not stern and severe, but responsive and get-at-able. With such a mother our boys will be gentle and our birds will be safe.

Try to think, boys, what a world this would be without any robins, or larks, or thrushes; without any songs in the apple trees getting all tangled up with the sunshine and the blossoms; without any canaries to sing in the window, or any meadow larks to whip out their flutes among the clover heads. If you should wake up some morning and experience the ghastly silence of a songless world you would want to hire somebody to thrash you that you ever used a sling-shot. Do you remember the minister down New York way whom they fined for shooting robins? I never wanted to get up on a mountain top so much in all my life and shout glory as I did over that verdict. I have heard of immorality among ministers, and I have heard of hypocrisy and lying and all sorts of offenses against good taste and morals, but I never heard of anything so contemptibly and causelessly mean as for one of God's especial teachers to get up in the morning, put on top boots, cross the river in the sunshine and dew of early morning, lift his gun, take deliberate aim and bring down a robin. If I was the Lord I would never forgive it. Men are not to blame sometimes when their blood gets too warm and they do impetuous things, but to deliberately descend to the ignominy of shooting a robin and calling it sport is to sink too low for justification.

Whatever else you be, boys, be brave. If you must sail in and fight, if your superfluous zeal is too much for you, go out in the field and square off at a bull. There is some glory in whipping anything bigger and stronger than yourself, but to show fight to a bird is a little too much like sneaking out and tripping up a cripple in the dark. I am going to write down a verse for you to write in your copy books this very day, and then good-night to you:

> "The bravest are the tenderest;
> The loving are the daring."

Isn't it heavenly to see the primrose around again? And the daffodils? And the hyacinths? Last night I went home with a rose in my button which cost me just five cents. At that rate, by careful abstaining from anything more expensive than a ten-cent lunch, one can go on wearing roses until next November. The robins have come back, too, and this morning a couple of them awoke me with their "Cheer-up" song. The indications are that they are prospecting for spring housekeeping. If the cat kills them I shall kill the cat. I shall close my eyes and do the deed in the name of mercy, for I detest cats, both two-legged and four-legged, and I love robins both feathered and human.

I wonder why it is that the average woman can walk and talk, breathe and laugh, suffer and cry, and finally die and be buried, and all the way through make such a botch of her life! Why is it that we fall in love, so many of us, just on the verge of a life that opens like a summer's day, and change that life thereby, as a June morning is changed when great clouds rush into the sky and obscure the sun? Why are girls so proud to parade an engagement ring upon their finger, when the diamond is too often the danger-light thrown out above the breakers? Now and then, about as rarely as one picks up a ruby on the highway, or finds an enchanted swan circling over the duck pond, there is a happy marriage—at least such is the popular inference—as to the absolute certainty of the statement, ask the skeleton closet. I have lived a varied sort of life. I have wandered to and fro over the earth to some extent; I have known a great many people, and have found happiness in many ways, but looking back over all the path to-night and turning my little bull's-eye lantern of experience up to the present moment, I can neither remember nor record a dozen truly happy marriages. What constitutes happiness? Peace. What brings peace? Content. Who is contented? Not you and not I. What man or woman of all whom we know can we bring out into the full light of day and say of them, "Behold the contented one! The restful one! The happy pair!" You, my dear, have attained the ambition of your youthful dreams. You have married a man who dresses you splendidly, who gives you diamonds and never murmurs when the bills come in. But are you happy? Do you never walk to and fro with the restless countess in the sad old ballad, dreaming of "Alan Percy?" Do you never, when all is still, go down into that cemetery where life's "might have beens" lie buried in graves kept green forever with your tears, and walk and dream alone? And you, my friend, have married the man of your choice. Is there nothing in the handsome exterior that palls a bit now and then when you find how sordid and meager the soul is behind the smile you used to think so charming? Do you never find scorn creeping into your heart in place of adoration when you mark the unpaid bills and the shiftless endeavor that strew his idle way? And you, sir, have a merry and a pretty wife and the world calls you a lucky fellow. How many know of the sharp tongue that underlies her laughter and the feather-filled head that never yet has donated an earnest thought to the domestic economy? And you, my good sir, have married a blue stocking in the old acceptance of the term. She can swing off a leader or make a speech on a rostrum at short notice, but how would you like to rise right up here, poor dear, and tell just what comfort lies in being mated to a superior being who busies herself with work which shall be remembered perhaps when the dust on the center table, the holes in your stockings, the discomfort of the larder, and the untidiness of the household are forgotten? And you, my good fellow, have married a woman of "good form." She never does an indiscreet thing. She is "icily faultless" and splendidly stupid. She has the neck of a swan, the arms of a goddess, the foot of a patrician, and the soul of a mouse! The scent of a wayside lilac, perhaps, is sadder than tears to you, old comrade, when you look back across the years and see again the sweet dead face of one you trifled with, or whom you deserted for this woman with heart and body of snow, a purse filled with gold and a brain filled with feathers.

There is entire hopelessness to many women in the blank monotony of life after youth is past. An emotional nature, mercurial and restless, full of aspirations and longings, as the trees this perfect month are full of blossoms, and, like the trees, bearing a thousand blooms to one fruition, finds the destiny prepared for it almost unendurable, and often longs for death that shall end all. Because poverty grinds and hosts of menial duties accumulate, because the walls of an unquiet home, made unlovely perhaps by skeletons that no skill can quite conceal, close like a dungeon upon hope and all the sweet promises of youth, bright natures grow morose and bitter, warm hearts chill into apathy and gloom, and sunny brows darken under the cloud of almost perpetual irritability and discontent. It is useless to preach sermons to such cases—as useless as to read a book of etiquette in a prison ward or comfort the victims of a railroad disaster with a treatise upon reform in the management of roads. The worn, the wasted, the erring, and the cruelly maimed lie thick about us. Our business is to encourage, to love, to bind up, and cheer. God, in His own time, shall lift the discontented head above the power of conspiring cares to vex. It is for us to lend a helping hand down here where the "slough of despond"is deepest. When tides forget to obey the moon, or leaves to answer the will of the wind, then, and not sooner, shall these restless hearts of ours learn to be still, whatsoever destinies confront, or limitations thwart. In looking upon the lives of some women, the mother of six children, for instance, who takes boarders and keeps no help; the widow supporting her little brood by endless drudgeries; the big-hearted woman in whom the frolicsomeness and wit of girlhood die hard amid the sordid miseries of a poverty-stricken life; the sensitive, poetic soul, doomed to uncongenial companionships and the criticisms and ridicule of the unfriendly—I am reminded of the score of eagles I saw lately, chained in a dusty inclosure of Central Park. With clipped wings, and grand, homesick eyes, they sat disconsolate upon their perches, and moped the hours away. Would any sane being have reviled those sorry beings for a lack of spirit? Would not the gentle-hearted spectator have proffered a handful of fresh leaves rather, and turned away in pity that sympathy could do no more?

For these unhappy sisters of mine, the discontented, yearning "Marthas," troubled with many cares, wherever my letter may find them between the great seas, I have a word of comfort in my heart to-day. In the first place, do not think, because you so often fall into irritability and impatient speech, that God despises you as a sinner. He understands, if friend, husband, or neighbor do not. Strive not to yield to fretfulness then, but, when overcome by it, remember always God understands it all. You may be able to see no light in all the shrouded way, no lifting of the shadow, no promise of the dawn; but rest assured, however long the probation, the infinite content of Heaven awaits us very soon, if we strive as much as lies within us to overcome the infirmities of our temper, and keep our faces set towards the shining of His love. I know, dear heart, indeed I do, that to-morrow and to-morrow are just alike to hopeless fancy—full of dish-washing, and drudging, and back-bending toil—that the sparkle and song of life were long ago merged in the humdrum beat of treadmill years; but through just this test is your character building—through just its hard process is shaping the conqueror's crown flashing with splendid light. As the root tarries in the dark mold to burst by-and-by into radiant bloom above it, so your poor life is hidden now to bloom to-morrow. You are not wicked because you sometimes murmur, but try and think so much of what is going to be that you shall forget what is. The Tender Heart above absolves your beaten spirit from willful sin, though you are sometimes swept away on currents of doubt and unfaith; but try and keep your eye fixed upon the headlight of His love, whatever currents drift you away. Remember how human parents deal with their children, and learn a lesson of God's dealings. If my little girl has the ear-ache, or any other tormenting ailment of childhood, do I stand over her and exact songs and smiles? And do you think that when God, for some good reason of his own, lays heavy burdens upon a life, He is going to demand unswerving sweetness of speech or ethereal mildness of temper? When I see one scrubbing who was fitted to adorn the drawing-room, washing dishes who was created an artist or a genius, darning small boys' linsey pants and homespun stockings who was intended by nature to reign the crowned priestess of some high vocation; when I mark the furrows and zigzag footprints that an army of besieging cares have left on the cheek that in girlhood outblushed the wayside rose, or note how the hands that once drew divinest music from obedient keys have twisted and warped in the performance of homely duties, I feel impelled to kiss the faded cheek with a love surpassing a lover's, to fold the poor hands in a reverent grasp, for I tell you, however often she may faint and falter by the way, however "fretty," and worn, and peevish she may become, the woman who perseveres in the performance of uncongenial duties, who struggles through the flatness of monotonous drudgeries, conquering adverse circumstances, poverty, and destiny, by patience, love, and Christian faith, is a heroine fit to rank with martyrs and saints. Remember, I am not talking to women who find the burdens hard to bear and do not bear them; to mere whimperers, who, because the road is full of stones, sit down and refuse to travel; but to the brave, true hearts who "press onward" although no rose blossoms and no bird sings, content to faithfully perform the task of life, hoping that the fullness of time shall read the riddle of incongruous destiny. I have seen the time when household work seemed newly cursed—the very dew of the primal malediction upon it; when to charge upon the dinner dishes, attack the lamps, or descend into the vortex of family patching, seemed to call for greater courage than average human nature possessed. And when I imagine that shrinking carried on through dry years of monotonous experience, the same formulas to be observed, the same distaste to be overcome throughout a lifetime of toil, yet no duty shirked, no obligation set aside, I wonder if Heaven holds a crown too bright for such faithful lives.

The time of the year for violets and also for tramps is drawing near. Did you ever stop and think just what it means to be a tramp? It means no work, no money, no home, no shelter, no friends. Nobody in all the world to care whether you live or die like a dog by the roadside. It means no heaven for such rags to crawl into, no grave to hide them out of sight and no hand stretched out in all the world to give the greeting and the good-by of love. It means nobody in all the world to feel any interest in you and no spot in all the world to call your own, not even the mud wherein your vagrant footprint falls, no prospect ahead, and no link unbroken to bind you to the past. I tell you, when we sit down and figure out just what the term means, it will not be quite so easy next time the wretched tramp calls at our door to set the dog upon him or turn him empty-handed away. Let them work, you say. Look here, my good friend, do you know how absolutely impossible a thing it is getting to be in this overcrowded country for even a willing man to find work? It used to be that "every dog had his day," but the dogs far outnumber the days in free America. I know well educated, competent men who have been out of employment for months and years. I know brave and earnest women, with little children to support, who have worn beaten paths from place to place seeking, not charity, but honest employment, and failed to find it. What chance is there for a ragged tramp when such as these fail? Remember, once in a while, if you can, that the most grizzled and wretched tramp that ever plodded his way to a pauper's grave was once a child and cradled in arms perhaps as fond as those that enfolded you and me. Remember that your mother and his were made sisters by the pangs of maternal pain, and perhaps in the heaven from which the saintly eyes of your mother are watching for you his mother is looking out for him. Perhaps—who knows?—the footfall of the ragged and despised tramp shall gain upon yours and find the gate of deliverance first, in spite of your money and your pride.

THE BROOK.

Lifting its chalice of sun-kissed foam
Far up the heights where the wild winds roam,
Weaving a web of shadow and sheen
In lowland meadows of dewy green.

Murmuring over the mossy stones,
In cool green dells where the gold bee drones,
Sudden and swift the showery fall,
Startling the wood bird's madrigal.

Orbing itself in a crystal lake
Set round with thickets of tangled brake,
In waveless calm, an emerald stone,
In the lap of the dusky forest thrown.

Rosemary and Rue.

Silver flakes of tremulous light
Showering down from the fields of night,
Where the great white stars like lilies glow—
Tossed on its tide as feathery snow.

Hastening onward through troubled ways,
Forgotten for aye its woodland days,
Sullen and silent its banks beside
The free brook wanders, a mighty tide.

Beyond where the forest's purple rim
Belts the horizon, hazy and dim,
Thundering down from the frowning steeps,
Into the arms of the sea it leaps.

Did it ever strike you, I wonder, this marvel of our individuality? Alone we are born, alone we live, alone we die, alone we pay the penalty or reap the reward of our evil or well doing. In the troubles that assail us we stand singly, however many councillors may flock to the door of our tent. Not one in all the world, the nearest, the dearest or the best, can bear one pang of life's experience for us, love us as they may. We often hear a mother say: "My child is so headstrong; she will not take my advice; she will go her own way." Of course she will, and she will not, simply because individual tact is the law of all experience. It is not being headstrong, it is merely fulfilling destiny.

In the fight we wage we do not fight by platoons or squads, under a common leader, a thousand at a charge. We enter the lists one by one and fight single handed. We choose our own colors and there is little of pageantry or show. When we fall we fall as travelers disappear who walk across a coast that is honeycombed with quicksand. We vanish, not in crowds like men who are jostled out of life by earthquakes or flooded like rats by tidal waves, but we slowly succumb to the inevitable in solitudes where only the stars watch us and the spaces of a dim, unsounded sea catch the fret of our mortal moan.

I have always thought that I should love to have the world come to an end, with a grand final bang, while I was yet living and sentient on the surface. I would like to be flashed out of being in the conglomerate of a mighty swarm, like the covey of birds a huntsman's rifle brings down or the multitude a Pompeiian doom overtakes. Such dying would be like riding out of an electric-lighted station, by the car full, rather than sneaking a place on the back platform like a tramp. But after all, death would not lose its awful individuality even then. Marshal the whole world, and aim a single bullet at a hundred million souls, with power to still use each pulse beat in the same rifle flash of time, yet each man would die alone.

There is one final lesson to be gained through the doleful contemplation of the world's flood-tide of sorrow, and that is the lesson of how to bear our troubles so as to react as little as possible upon those with whom life throws us in daily contact. Because the goblin bee has stung our own souls, shall we seek to share the pain of its stateless sting with all we meet? No more than we should endeavor to carry contagion in our garments or put poison in our neighbor's well. I knew a man once, a gallant, light-hearted soldier, who honored the blue and brass of his country's uniform by wearing it. An awful sorrow suddenly smote his life, like an Indian sortie from an ambush. Wife and children were swept from his arms by a swift disaster and he was left alone. His friends said: "He is a wrecked man! He will never lift his head again!"

How did he fulfill this prophecy of woe? He entered the chamber of his darkened home and denied himself to everyone. He neither ate nor slept. He fought by himself a greater battle than call of bugle ever summoned to any field. He mastered his own soul, and emerged from that chamber after a certain number of days a conqueror over his own sorrow. His smile was as ready, his heart as tender, his genial speech as welcome at home and abroad as it had ever been, and only when the goblin bee of memory stung him in the silence of the companionless night did he live over again the experience of his sorrow. None knew when that sting came, or how it tarried; he bore it silently like a soldier and a man. The trifling world called him light of love and easily consoled, but I think he was a grand, unselfish hero, a benefactor rather than a destroyer of mankind.

When we get so that we can hide our sorrow in a smile we attain that attitude that brings us closest to the divine. The man or the woman who goes up and down the ways of the world with a groan on his lips and a weed on his arm is an infliction worse than an out of tune hand organ. If the bee stings, hold still and bear the hurt by yourself as best you may, but don't talk it over with everyone you meet, like an old woman petitioning a recipe for a bad cough and flaunting her physical ailments forever in your face. When you have bright things to talk about and comforting things to say, talk; otherwise hold your peace. The reason, I think, why animals are never wrinkled and drawn of feature and gray like mankind is because they cannot talk. If they had the power of speech they would go around as humans do and disseminate unpleasant topics, as idle winds start thistle pollen. Silence is golden when you can find nothing better to do than to clamor your own troubles; speech only is blessed when, like a bird, it evolves a song or wings a feathered hope.

It seems hardly the thing to do, perhaps, to single out the unhappy folks in a present world so full of jollity and talk with them awhile to-day. This bright autumn weather is so crowded with sights and sounds to dazzle and enchant that to obtrude the leaf of rue within the garland or breathe a minor tone into the music seems almost out of place. And yet, for some reason or other, as I sit here at my desk to-day, the thought of the hearts that are heavy in the midst of all the world's fair pageant, and the eyes that cannot see the banners by reason of their tears, come to me with a strong and resistless force.

Alas, for the goblin bee that stings, yet all too often may not "state its sting"! We walk with a crowd, and yet are conscious that our way is not theirs. It lies apart, we know not why, and evermore dips into shadow and threads the dark defiles of gloom. There are so many more reasons for being sorry than for being glad, we think. Try to count the causes for laughter, and then, over against them, set the reasons for sorrow and see which way the balance falls. I take my seat on a bench out at the big show and watch the crowd for an hour. Do I see many faces that do not bear the scar of the "goblin bee"? From the little four-year-old who is bitterly crying because somebody has jostled its toy from its hand, to the woman whose eyes are sunken with sorrow because death has jostled the one whom she loved into his grave, everybody who passes, with but few exceptions, shows the scar of that stateless sting.

Look at my window-garden, yonder! The sunshine, stealing in from the south, has wooed a dozen pansies into bloom—"Johnny-jump-ups," they used to call them when I was a girl. How bright and cheery and chatty they look. We have those sort of faces (some of us) every day about our breakfast tables. The little folks, God bless 'em! with their shining hair, their bright eyes, and the soft velvet of their cheeks, are the blessed heartsease of our home. And there is a fuchsia, turbaned like a Turk, behind the pansies. Just such sumptuous, graceful women we see every day. Like the fuchsia, they are beautiful and that is all. They yield no fragrance. They attract the eye but fail to reach the heart. Who wouldn't rather have mignonette growing in the window? There is a yellow blossom in the window that reminds one of the patient shining of certain homely souls I know, making sunshine in humble homes; cheerful old maid aunts, sweet-hearted elder sisters, yielding the honey of their hearts to others. A cluster of fading violets sets me thinking of frail invalids and the host of "shut-in" ones, whose delicate and dying beauty fills our eyes with unstayed tears and our hearts with the shadow of coming sorrow.

There are gates that swing within your life and mine from day to day, letting in rare opportunities that tarry but a moment and are gone, like travelers bound for points remote. There is the opportunity to resist the temptation to do a mean thing; improve it, for it is in a hurry, like a man whose ticket is bought and whose time is up. It won't be back this way, either, for opportunities for good are not like tourists who travel on return tickets. There is the opportunity to say a pleasant word to your wife, sir, or you, madam, to your husband, instead of venting your temper and your "nerves" upon each other. Love's opportunity travels by lightning express and has no time to dawdle around the waiting-room. If you improve it at all it must be while the gate swings to let it through.

My dear, let me implore you, whatever else you let go, hold on to your enthusiasm. Grow old if you must; grow white-headed and bent and care-furrowed, if such must needs be the process of years, but don't grow to be a stick. If you must pass on from the green time of your freshness, change into sweet hay and keep your fragrance. If the cage must grow rusty and lose its brightness, there is a bird within, that it were a pity to strangle to keep it from singing to the end. I don't care how successful, or rich, or learned a man becomes, if he maintains a grim repression of all romance and enthusiasm, and what some hard old "Gradgrinds" call the "nonsense" within him, he is nothing more than a fine cage with a dead bird in it. When I hear a person say of another, "Oh, he is a substantial fellow; no nonsense about him!" I picture a gold-fish in a glass globe. A glittering cuticle that covers anything so bloodless as the anatomy of a fish is not worth much. There are a good many types of men to be detected, but the bloodless, emotionless, heart-paralytic, is the worst. Polish up a golden ball all you like. It may ornament your mantel, or serve as a useless bit of glitter in some corner, but when you begin to feel hungry and faint, and in need of solace and cheer, you will turn from the golden ball and pick up the veriest old rusty coat apple from an orchard's windfall, that has mellowed under summer noon, and sweetened in summer rains and dews, praising God for its flavor and its juices, even if you can buy forty bushels of its counterpart, for the price of one of your polished golden balls. Cultivate the "nonsense" in you, then, if it tends to enthusiasm of the right sort. It is the sympathy we get from people, the heartsomeness and cheer that keep our souls nourished, rather than the mere dazzle of intellectual attainment, or the greatness of any worldly achievement. Heart rather than head; nature rather than art; genuineness rather than pretense; romance rather than absolute realism; enthusiasm rather than petrifaction, will make a man rather than a gold fish, a juicy apple rather than a ball of metallic and glittering nothingness.

We were gathered at the Norfolk Station awaiting the train that was to carry us over the marshes to Virginia Beach and the sea. The crowd that surrounded us was very different from a Chicago crowd. There was no pushing, no bold assertiveness, no elbows. There were lots of pretty women, and as for me everybody knows I simply adore the open sky, a tree in blossom and a pretty woman. There were young girls with velvety brown eyes within whose dusky shadows one might look fathom deep as into a well of limpid water; girls with blue eyes like fringed gentians; women with grand free curves of figure that would have made Hebe look commonplace; women with shapely shoulders and long, aristocratic hands, tinted at the finger-tips as though fresh from picking ripe strawberries; girls all in white (for the day was warm), like June lilies; women with snowy teeth and adorable smiles to disclose them; little tots of girls with braided hair and soft, questioning eyes; queenly girls, like tulips in bloom, all chatting together in subdued but merry tones and laughing as delicately and airily as thrushes sing. Oh, I lost my heart to you, my pretty southern maidens, and count the time well spent I devoted to the contemplation of your many graces away down in that little station by the torrid bay.

If I was a liar and wanted to reform I shouldn't quit lying all at once. I would start out with a covenant to occasionally tell the truth. By and by this spasmodic truth-telling, like the grain blown by the wind among stones, would, perhaps, yield sufficient harvest to send me not quite empty-handed up to St. Peter's gate. If I drank whisky I would commence to reform by swearing off on one glass out of three, and perhaps the manhood within me, having so much more chance to grow, would elbow its way into heaven. If I was a gossip I would try to hold my tongue from speaking evil half the time, and in that blissful interval perhaps my dwarfed soul would get a start skyward. It is not by sudden achievement that we consummate a long journey. It is step by step and mile by mile over a stony road that brings us to the goal, and it is not by mere resolving that we renounce the old and attain unto the new. He who travels but a few steps and keeps his face heavenward is on the way, and every small decision for the right, faithfully adhered to, is a notable step toward a consummated journey.

I am often struck with the selfishness displayed by people who are fortunate enough to be provided with umbrellas in time of sudden showers. They calmly behold hosts of unhappy beings battling their way through the storm, drenched to the bone, and with ruined garments, yet never think of saying, "Accept a share of my umbrella," or "Walk with me as far as our ways lie together." If I should hear such a speech I might drop senseless with surprise, but all the same I should hail it as the bugle note that heralded a new era of courteous kindness.

We are not put into the world to be suspicious of one another. We were put here to make the world pleasanter for our tarrying, and to cultivate a fellowship with souls. If the guests at a mountain inn, sojourning together for a stormy night, spend the time in reviling one another, or in calling attention to each other's blemishes, we write them down as snobs; but what shall we call the tenants of transitory time who spend the span of mortal life in doing all they can to make one another uncomfortable? We have only a watch in the night to tarry together; let us try to make that hour a profitable one and a pleasant memory for others when we have journeyed on.

I have often wondered how Christian people got round the gospel command, "Love thy neighbor as thyself." It doesn't say love him (or her) after a proper introduction, or if agreeable, or congenial, or of good family and established reputation—it simply gives the command on general principles. I don't pretend to be good enough to obey the mandate myself, for I honestly think it is a species of hypocrisy to say you love everybody. One might as well say one were fond of all fruit alike, whether specked, wormy or rotten. But let my good orthodox professor put this in his pipe and smoke it. Let him remember it next time he sees his neighbor plunged into an extremity, or handicapped by an annoyance of any kind. If we love our neighbor we are bound to help him, and neighbor in this sense means any-one who chances to be near us, whether black or white, raggedly disreputable or sanctimoniously frilled.

Rosemary and Rue.

There is more selfishness perpetrated in the world under guise of family ties than in almost any other way. The man who does good and unselfish deeds only for his own children and for the immediate circle housed beneath his roof, forgetful of the claims of the great, tormented, harassed and struggling world, is a selfish man and accountable to heaven for a great deal of meanness. I don't care how much he puts on his children's backs, or how many luxuries he surrounds them with, the Lord will not hold him guiltless if he does nothing for the stranger who tugs by him in the stress of life's uncertain weather, or for the neighbor who sits disconsolate outside his gates.

I wish that vagabond and his dog who were brought before a west side justice yesterday for vagrancy would travel up my way. I like that sort of thing that leads a man to be faithful to his dog. It goes without saying that the dog is faithful to the man, but it is not often that the master shows the same spirit to the fond and steadfast brute. If the two should journey my way I think they would have one white day in the calendar. Good heavens, my dear, do you ever stop long enough in the midst of your golf-playing and your tennis tournaments, your yachtings and your outings to think what it is to be a tramp? To be unable to find a stroke of work; to be sick and starved and homeless! Like "poor Joe," to be told to "move on" every time you stop to rest; to eat the grudgingly given crust of charity, and have no friend under the sun, moon or stars but a flea-bitten dog? Did you ever stop to think, my Christian friend, that that tramp is a neighbor whom you are to love? And if you are going to love him I will love his dog! No doubt the latter is the better man of the two.

Did you ever read of a battle siege in olden times? There were the full-armored warriors, resplendent in shining metal and plumed crests; there were the mighty battering rams, and the flash of battle axes, the thunder of advancing feet and the trumpet call before the gates. But more potent than all else in the doomed city's destruction was the secret work of the sappers and miners—the patient forces which wrought their work out of sight and hearing. And

I have been thinking to-night, as I sit here, where the firelight weaves its delicate tapestry within the beautiful walls of home, that it is not going to be the pompous ones who shall march triumphant at last into the "City of Gold," but they who have worked patiently and humbly out of sight and with no meed of praise. The man who has held to the dictates of his own conscience, not conforming to the company he marched with; the man who has dared to be himself in a world where men are labeled in lots; the man who has held it high honor to suffer for a principle or to be loyal to an unpopular friend or cause; the man who has erected a standard made up between his own heart and heaven, and, independent of the world's verdict of praise or blame, followed it to the end, is going to wear a crown by and by, when the epauletted general and the pompous staff are forgotten. Prayer is not always a genuflexion and an address. It is oftener hard work. The farmer praying at his weeds, the pilot praying from every spoke of his wheel, the mother whose daily life of unselfish toil and far-reaching influence is a prayer, do more to stir the divine heart, to keep the world's prow headed for heaven than half the solicitations or apologetic addresses made in our churches under the name of prayer.

When you and I get rich, my dear, as some day we surely shall, what are we going to do with all our money? We will hunt up some of the improvident ones, those who could never make the two ends meet, those who through good heartedness, or lack of forethought or unselfish desire to make other folks happy, have never laid by a cent, and we will give those silly people such a good time they will carry its impress all through their after lives, as a pat of butter carries the print. We will slyly pay the bills for improvident ones who have grown gray in the effort to make a decent funeral for dead horses. They shall forget how to spell "care" and their new and happy dialect shall know no such words as "monthly payments," "righteous dues" or "can't afford it." I am convinced that as a rule it is not the sweet-hearted people who take on this world's gain. There is many a poor beggar with not a change of linen to his back who would make a more royal host, had the smiling face of fortune turned his way, than the rightful owner of the vast estates at whose gate he stands and begs. The big hearts too often go with the empty purse, and the little, wizened, skin-flint souls, that it would take a thousand of to crowd the passage through the eye of a needle, gain all the golden favors of the god of plenty.

After dinner I said to the little folks, "Behold, I will buy me a pair of stockings and hire a bathing suit, and the afternoon shall be devoted to frolic and thee." So we went to the small booth, where an exceedingly meek young man sold ginger pop and fancy shells, and paralyzed him with a demand for ladies' hose. He didn't know what we meant until I came out boldly and unblushingly and asked for women's stockings. He said he didn't keep 'em. "Have you a mother?" said I. "No." "Have you a sister? Or is there a nearer one yet and a dearer, from whom I could buy or borrow a pair of stockings that I may go in bathing?" He didn't understand that either, but finally, with the aid of lucre, I made the matter clear so that he got me a pair of canary-striped woolen hose, evidently laid by for some farmer's winter use, and I bought them for a sum that made his eyes grow dim with rapture. We went down to the beach, and after a season of prayer with the young person to induce her to put on some horrid tights, we all went in and enjoyed such a dip as only salt water yields. In the midst of it we had to go on shore several times to stand the boy on his head and pump the ocean out of him, as he was constantly getting drowned in the surf, and one of my expensive and expansive stockings was captured out at sea and brought back by a son of Belial, who seemed greatly affected by its size, but in spite of such small drawbacks we had a glorious time.

"What is the matter, my darling?" asked John, the newly married, to the wife of his bosom.

"Nothing whatever," replied Mrs. John.

"But you look like a funeral," exclaimed he.

"I am not aware that I look more than usually unamiable; I certainly never felt better," replied his wife, placidly folding down meanwhile the hem to a distracting little apron she is making. John seizes his hat, pushes it down over his eyes and rushes forth distracted with the conjecture as to what terrible thing he has been guilty of to make his wife look so like an injured martyr. For the time being love is dead, joy wiped from the face of the earth, hope crucified and peace assassinated, all because of bottled thunder. A word would have explained all, a look has ruined everything.

"Don't put on your fresh muslin this afternoon," suggests the prudent mother.

"But why not?" replied the sprightly Jane; "it is the only endurable dress this warm weather."

"Oh, very well, do as you like, of course," meekly replied the parent in a tone that suggests a serpent's fang, a hoary head and a broken heart all in one.

Now, in my opinion it is not conducive to domestic harmony to have too much of this sort of repression. It is like living in an exhaust chamber. One would be certain to choke up and burst very soon. Self-control does not consist in forever keeping one's mouth shut, alone. A look, a sneer, a drooping mouth, a tilted nose, will do as much mischief as a loosened tongue. Why I should go about like a disagreeable old martyr or like a sneering Saul of Tarsus, and call myself pleasant to live with, simply because I don't talk, is something not easily understood.

I would far rather be a target for flying saucepans every time I popped my head into the kitchen than have a cook there who never says a word, but is sullen and ugly enough to carve me up like cold meat. I would rather be a constant attendant at funerals, a nurse in a fever-ward, a girl in a circus, or a street car horse, than live with proper folks who never make blunders, or commit indiscretions either of speech or manner, but look at you every time you sneeze as though your featherheadedness was the only thing that made life unbearable. Out with it then if you have cause for offense. Don't let the clouds hang a single hour, but turn on the weather faucet and let it rain. If your neighbor has insulted you, either ask her why or ignore it. Ten to one the fancied insult is only a wind cloud, and sunshine will break it away. If you feel mad sail right in for a tempest and have done with it. Thunder and lighten, blow and hail if you want to, but don't be a non-committal dog-day. Bottled thunder is a bad thing to keep on the family shelves. It is likely to turn sour on your hands, and before you get through with it, you will wish you had died young.

Yonder goes a small and worthless yellow dog. He is young; you can tell that from the abnormal size of his paws, and a certain remnant of wistful trust in human kind, which displays itself in the furtive wag of his tail and the cock of his limp and discouraged ear. He is as absolutely friendless as anything to which God has granted life can be. Of his existence there is no thought in the mind of any man or woman beneath the stars. The boys grow mindful of him now and then, though, and their manifested interest has made of his life one terrible specter of cringing fear. He hears the hurrah of their cruel chase in every tone of sudden speech; he sees the menace of a blow in every shadow. Do you know, my dear, that I never spoke a truer word in all my life than when I say that underneath the hide of that forlorn and friendless little yellow dog there is something more valuable than beats under the broadcloth vests and silken waists of many of the men and women who pass him by! A grateful heart mindful of the smallest kindnesses, a faithful instinct which keeps dogs loyal even to cruel masters. I sometimes think I would rather take my chances with honest dogs than with half the men who own them. They may not be able to pass up the stamped ticket which transfers the human passenger from the earthly to the celestial railroad and carries him through on the passport of an immortal soul; but no ticket at all is quite as good as a forged or fraudulent one, as some of us will find out, I am thinking, when we hand up our worthless checks!

Which would you rather be in the orchestra of human life, a flute or a trombone? To be sure, the latter is heard the farthest, but the quality of the flute tone reaches deeper down into the soul and awakens there dreams without which a man's life is like bread without leaven, or a laid fire without tinder. I don't like noisy people, do you? People who talk and bluster and swagger. People who remind us of bladders filled to the point of explosion with wind. We like sensitive people, quiet-voiced, deep-hearted, earnest people, with the quality of the flute rather than that of the fog-horn in their make-up. And yet how much greater demand there is for bluster than there is for force. Sometimes I am inclined to think that life is a farce played with an earthly setting for the delectation of the angels, as we serve minstrel shows and burlesques. It isn't the shy and the timid who get the applause; the clown in tinsel and the end man in cork divide easy honors. And yet, thank God for flutes! Thank God the orchestra isn't entirely composed of trombones and bass drums.

WHAT I MISS.

I can get used to my darling's dress
   That hangs on the closet door;
And the little silent half-worn shoes
   That patter no more on the floor.

I can get used to the hopeless blank
  That greets my waking eyes,
As they meet the sight of the empty crib
  Where no little nestling lies.

I can get used to the dreary hush,
  In the home which my darling blest
With her prattling speech and her rippling laugh,
  Ere we laid her away to rest.

But, ah! the touch of those little hands
  That wandered o'er my face,
Like the wavering fall of rose-leaves soft,
  In some sunlit garden place.

Those dimpled caressing baby hands!
  I feel them again at night,
And in dreams I gather them back again
  From their harp in the City of Light.

My hungry heart will claim them still;
  I cannot let them depart.
So I gather them back again in dreams
  To my desolate, breaking heart.

The other day my strolling took me into a second-hand furniture shop. I wanted to find an ice chest. "Have you any second-hand chests?" I asked of the hoary-headed son of Erin who tended the place and raked in the shekels. He didn't answer a word, but silently arose and beckoned me to follow. Through ranks of withered tables and blighted chairs I picked my way until my guide dived down a gruesome stairway and then I stopped. Presently his head emerged like a grimy Jack-in-the-box.

"Is it an ice chist yez want?" asked he. There was mold on his faded cheeks and a cobweb on his brow as he awaited my answer.

"Must I go down there to find it?" I inquired. He replied in the affirmative.

"Old man, I will go no further," said I, "but come back here and tell me the price of this lovely desk." So saying, I designated a delightful old claw-handled, brass-mounted, spider-legged piece of furniture, which might have been used by Adam to cast up his accounts on. There was a suggestion of secret drawers about it that was quite ravishing. The doors were oddly shaped little panes of mirror glass, within which I gazed pensively at a soot blemish on my nose. "Is it the price of that yez'd be afther knowing?" said the old man, in the tone of one who dealt with a harmless lunatic. "I thought it was ice chists yez was afther." "Yes," said I, drawing out two long slabs as I spoke, such as were used to support the shelf of the desk I remembered in my grandmother's house. "That bit of furnichoor," said the old man, gazing sadly meanwhile at the grime of ages which I could not rub from off my nose, "is more than two hundred years old." He stopped for a moment to see if I would believe him, then went on: "Yis, ma'am, that same is nearer three hundred years old, all told."

Here I gave him a look which stopped him at the threshold of the fourth century.

"Yez may have it for $25," says he.

"I'll give you five," says I.

He turned away as one who found his mother tongue inadequate to express the deep-seated scorn of his soul. I followed.

"Did yez say twenty?" he asked stopping abruptly and facing me with the blurred photograph of what was once an engaging smile.

"I said five," I answered.

"Well, take it thin," said he, "but it would be dirt chape at fifty. It's not a day less than four hun—"

"Stop," said I, "if you add another century I'll only pay you two and a half for it."

And so to-night it comes to pass that I am writing at my new old desk. I am half conscious, as my pencil glides along the paper, of a laughing face, half-hidden by showers of falling hair, that flickers like a shadow in and out of the soft gloom that enfolds me. Fingers, light as air, seem to follow the motion of my own, and the ghost of the mistress who thought and wrote at this same desk, one, two, three, four hundred years ago, seems whispering in my ear. I wonder what will be the effect if I read to that sweet, gentle woman of "ye olden time" a few bits from the morning paper.

Madam, are you aware that a man kicked his wife to death yesterday because she failed to have his supper ready for him? Are you not to be congratulated that you are out of reach of this latter day development of the human brute? Do you know that the Blank concerts began this last week, and that the melodies that throng the beautiful hall yonder on the avenue are like bands of singing angels charming a world's sorrows to rest? Do not the gentle caprices of the flutes and the swing of the fiddles make even you, flake of airy nothingness that you are! dance like a thistledown in a summer breeze? Madam, do you know, and how does it affect you to know, that there are bargain sales in town where you can buy a gown for a song, and a pair of all-wool blankets for the worth of a dream? In your long time disembodied state have you yet reached a point, I wonder, when such news as this can no longer thrill a woman's heart? If so, madam, you are truly and undeniably dead, and your room is better than your company. I bid you a gentle good evening.

Among the many things I shall be glad to find out some day will be why, in spite of heroic effort to keep it straight, my hat always gets crooked and my hair becomes disordered on the march. I thoroughly detest the sight of a typical "blue-stocking," or a literary woman who affects a sublime superiority to appearances, and yet Mrs. Jellyby was nowhere as to general demoralization of raiment compared to my unfortunate self. Taking my seat in a down-town restaurant the other day, I found myself surrounded by half a dozen girls as bright and pretty and jolly as girls go. No sooner was I seated than the whisper went round that a newspaper woman had invaded the party. "Looks like one," murmured the plumpest one of the lot, and I could have cried. "Girls," I wanted to say, "judge not by appearances. The best christians sometimes have red noses, just as the jolliest literary folks have frowsy hair and abandoned hats. They can't help it, my dears, any more than a black cat can help being somber. It is never safe to condemn anybody, not even a poor, miserable scribbler for the press, on circumstantial evidence. You see a crooked hat, electric hair, and that is all. Put on Titbottom spectacles and look deeper. Perhaps you will then see an anguish-stricken woman rising at 5 a. m. to make herself smart for the day. You will note how carefully she adjusts the feeble adjuncts to her toilet, how she places her hat on straight and secures it with a cast-iron cable! How she combs out her curls and sticks a feathery kerchief within her belt. Two hours later the cable hat-pin has been struck by a tidal-wave and swept from its anchorage; the curls have degenerated into wisps of wind-tossed hay;

and the kerchief? Gone as a feather is gone when the summer tempest gets behind it! We mean well, girls. We want to look trim and slick and span. All of us poor literary people do, but we can't bring it about. Life is so everlastingly full, anyway, that it seems preposterous to spend more than half one's time in getting fixed up. Sometimes I am foolish enough to believe that good St. Peter, when we come toiling up to his gate, won't look so much to the condition of our hats and our hair as he will to the way we wear our souls. If they are tip-tilted and frowsy it may go a little bit hard with us. Of course, it is a good thing to be able to wear a hat straight, and be remarked for your pretty hair and generally pleasing appearance, but I declare to you if it comes to a question of mental array and soul-correction as opposed to style and good form, I am willing to choose the former and be laughed at now and then by saucy girls."

That's right. Stand on shore and beat him back when he attempts to make a landing. If necessary, club him under water and congratulate yourself that you are so self-righteous and everlastingly holy that nobody can get a chance to swing a club at you. What is this half-dead thing that is trying to force its way onto dry land from the whelming waters of temptation and misery? A rat? Oh, no; only a human creature like yourself. Sin overtaken and subdued by evil. He is young, perhaps, and never had a mother's care or a father's training. He has drifted with easy currents into dangerous waters, and the devil, who lurks beneath the flood, is trying to snatch him down to hell! Raise your club and give him a clip! The audacity of such a boy trying to be anything with such a record behind him! Oh, I am sick of you all, you omniverous feeders on reputation, you unveilers of past records of shame! I hope in my heart that if ever you get your own foot on the threshold of some haven of relief, after a tight tussle with danger and death, an angel will stand over against the doorway with a flaming sword and demand to see your credentials. No hope of that, though. Angels are not up to that sort of work; it is left to men, and sometimes—God pity us all!—to women.

If you expect to escape criticism, girls, in this world, you will put yourselves very much in the plight of flower-roots that expect to grow without the discipline of the hoe. Before we can amount to anything either in blossom or as fruit, we must undergo much honest criticism, and of such we need never be afraid. A candid and above-board enemy is of far more benefit, often, than a timid friend, who, seeing our faults, is afraid to tell us of them. The fact that boys stone certain trees and pass others by, is explained when we find that the stones are always thrown at the fruit-bearing trees. And so with character; the fact that we are criticized proves that we are something better than scrub-oak saplings. But all criticism that does not make us grow, and put forth fairer and richer blossoms, is like a hoe made of wood, or a cultivator without power applied to cause it to destroy the weeds. If the unanimous verdict of the community in which we live asserts that we are proud, or ill-natured, or lazy, we may be pretty sure that there is some cause for the application of that particular stroke of the hoe, and the sooner we set about seeking to remedy the evil, the better for our next world's crop of blossoms. Nobody (save One) was ever yet maligned without some little cause. Those who come in contact with you at home may not see little blemishes upon your conduct or character which those who meet you in business may detect. For instance, to the folks at home you never put on that indifferent and languid air to which you treat the customer who drops in to buy ribbon, or the woman who asks you a question at your office desk. The customer and the questioner go away with an estimate of your behavior very unlike the one held at home, where you are frank and cheerful, and willing to please. And, on the other hand, the party with whom you associate casually in business, or with whom you ride daily to and from your office and your home, has no conception how snappy and snarly you can be when none but familiar ears are open to your surly complaints.

The statement from your little brother or sister that you are a "cross old thing" would hardly be believed by those who meet you away from home. And yet the hoe in the little hands strikes at a weed that threatens to make havoc in the garden. Better look to it, dearie, before the ugly thing quite overtops the mignonette and the pinks! Whenever you hear of an adverse criticism set to find the weed somewhere in your character. I believe firmly that every one of us was born into the world with capabilities for almost every evil under the sun if environment favors the development. Like a garden patch, the roots of the weeds lie already deep, the flower seeds must be sown. And no gardener ever struggled with "pusley" and burdock as we must struggle with the evil crop, heredity-sown. Thanks be to the quick eye, then, be it of friend or foe, who discerns the weed before we do, and whips out the hoe to attack it. We are not exactly pleased when it is borne in upon us through the criticism of some acquaintance or neighbor, that we are selfish in little things. Our folks don't say so, and we try to believe the charge is a libel. Next time you throw your banana skin heedlessly on the pavement, or crowd into a seat without a "by your leave," or refuse to move up in a crowded car, or open your window without asking if it be agreeable to the person behind you, or eat peanuts and throw the shucks on the floor instead of out of the window, or see a lady going by with a disarranged dress and don't tell her of it, or return an indifferent answer to a civil question, or refuse the sweet service of a smile and a gentle look to the humblest wayfarer that jostles you on the road, just remember the criticism, and see if there is not occasion for it. Set about correcting the little faults, and the great ones leave to God. He will keep you, no doubt, from theft, and murder, and perjury, but you don't ask or seem to stand in need of His help in getting rid of temptations to be mean and selfish, and discourteous and lazy.

What would you think of a gardener who went about with a spade seeking to exterminate nothing but Canada thistles, and let all the rest of the weeds go? It is not often that so big and determinate a thing as a Canada thistle gets in among the roses, and when it does it is quickly disposed of. But oh, the wee growths! The tiny shoots that come up faster than flies swarm in dog-days, and need to be forever stood over against with a steady hand and a hoe. If my neighbor comes out and charges me with stealing a barrel of flour from her storehouse, or attacking her first-born with a meat-axe, I can quickly disprove that sort of a charge; but when she says that I am unprincipled because I steal in and coax her girl away from her with the offer of higher wages—how is that? Or that I am selfish because she sees me let my old mother wait on me to what I am able to get myself; or cross, because I am untender to the children; or untruthful, because I instruct the servant to say I am "not at home" when I am, how am I going to dispose of those charges? Sure as you live, there are weeds in front of such hoe strokes, and with heaven's help we'll get rid of 'em.

Cultivate your critics, then, provided they be honest and fair-dealing. Avoid only such as strike in the dark. The man who goes out to hoe weeds in the night time is not to be trusted, and the enemy who resorts to the underhand methods of backbiting and scandal to do his work, is not worth talking about, much less heeding. Take criticism that is fair and open, as you occasionally take quinine, to tone up the system and dissipate the malaria of sloth and inertia. Only they shall come into the festival by and by, bearing garlands of roses, and wreaths of hearts' delight and balm, who have welcomed the strong stroke of the hoe at the root of every blossom to bear down the weeds and loosen the tough and sun-baked soil.

As Charles Kingsley says:

"My fairest child, I have no song to give you;
   No lark could pipe 'neath skies so dull and
     gray;
Yet, ere we part, one lesson I can leave you
   For every day:

"Be good, sweet maid, and let who will be
   clever;
Do noble things, not dream them, all day long,
And so make life, death and that vast forever
   One grand, sweet song."

See that half-grown man? He never will know as much again as he does now at the ripe age of twenty. When he gets to be fifty, when his hair is grizzled and his hopes are like the dead leaves that cling to November trees, he will look back upon these years of rare wisdom and colossal effrontery and blush a little, perhaps, at the recollection. Now he has no reverence for a woman or for God. He sneers at good in a world whose threshold he has barely crossed, as a year-old child might stand in the doorway of his nursery and denounce what was going on in the drawing-room. Most of the scathing things that are said about domestic felicity, and the sneers that are bestowed on love, and the gibes that are flung at purity, and the scoffs that are launched at established religions; all the jokes at the expense of noble womanhood and the witticisms that are lavished upon the old-fashioned virtues, spring from the gigantic brain of the youth of the period.

Often as I pass along the streets of this town I notice certain places which I do not burn down, nor tear down, nor otherwise demolish, merely because of inherent cowardice and inadequate strength. If I had a wide-awake, growing boy I would no more turn him loose in your town, Mr. Alderman, than I would cut his throat with my own hand. Not, certainly, if there was a spark of human nature within him, and a boy without such a spark is hardly worth raising. And more than that, I will say this, that what with your saloons and your wide-open gambling resorts, and your doorways of hell, wherein sit spiders luring flies, it has come to pass that every mother whose boy encounters harm thereby should be entitled to damages at least as great as juries award a careless pedestrian who gets his legs cut off at a railway crossing. You say that laws are inadequate to cope with evils of this kind; if that is so, then an outraged citizenhood should rise superior to law, and enter upon a crusade to destroy the infamous dens that decoy our boys. On a certain downtown street there is a newly opened resort, the windows of which are closely draped, and before the door of which a placard is suspended which invites only men to enter within. Now and then a hideously ugly man, with a yellow beard, comes to the ticket window and looks out like a tarantula from its hole, but in the main the place seems absolutely unfrequented.

Take your stand and watch for awhile, though, and you will see young men and small boys, old men and slouching reprobates of all conditions and colors going in and coming out by dozens. Why doesn't some good citizen enter a complaint of that place and break it up? We would pounce upon a smallpox case soon enough wherever it might lurk, but we are strangely indifferent where the menace is only to the soul.

How can we expect to keep our boys pure and raise them to lives of usefulness when such iniquitous places are run wide open on public streets at noonday, granting admission to all masculinity between the ages of 7 and 70?

A well-guarded youth is supposed to be at home in the night time and not to be frequenting shy neighborhoods at any hour. So that we might feel comparatively safe about the boy we send out into the world at an early age to begin his career as errand boy or messenger if these pernicious decoys were maintained only at night and in low vicinities. When the trap is set, however, right in the business center of the town by daylight, what safety have we? Whenever I look into the face of an eager, bright, curious, thoroughly alive boy I feel like shaking every other duty of life and going forth to do battle with the devil for that lad's soul.

Why should evil have so much greater chance than good? For one reason I don't believe we make the good attractive enough. The devil has stolen the trademark of light for half his wares. Why not have more fun and frolic in the home? Why not add a gymnasium and dancing hall to the Sunday school and filter some of the world's innocent sunshine inside its gloomy walls? Why may not the eager, active heart of youth find its good cheer and jollity somewhere else than in forbidden places and among smooth and unscrupulous knaves? If we made our churches less austere and their gatherings more alluring to the young, these low and vicious resorts might close for lack of patronage.

God bless the boys. I love them next best to girls, and sometimes even a little better, when they are especially frank and brave and true. I am not going to see them harmed without a protest, either, and I would be one of a crowd this very day to march upon the resorts of evil that lie in wait, all over town, to destroy the bonnie fellows. If I had my way, every man or woman who makes money by pandering to the curiosity of a boy's nature, inciting to unworthy passion by means of lewd pictures and the like, should be consigned to instant perdition. The earth is too hallowed to receive their vile dust!

Dear girls, if you would be beautiful with the beauty that strikes root in heaven, first of all be natural. Be true to something within you higher than any conventional code or worldly wise mandate. If it is your natural impulse to be courteous, and sympathetic, and sweet (and blessed be the fact, it is the natural impulse of most girls so to be!), don't let miserable conformity and its tricksters exchange your genuine blossom for a mere shred of painted muslin, fashioned though it be after even so perfect a similitude of a rose. The birds of the air nor the angels in heaven will ever be fooled by any artificial rose, let me tell you, however much dudes and society feather-heads may pretend to desire it. Grow for something better than this world; wear your sweetness in your heart rather than on your pocket handkerchief.

The great drawback to domestic felicity often lies in the fact that we get too familiar with one another. There should be a certain reserve in the most intimate relationships. Sisters and brothers have no right to burst into one another's private rooms without knocking. Wives have no more right to search their husband's pockets than they have to do the same little service for a distant acquaintance. I have no right to read the Young Person's letters without permission, although I have a right to win her confidence so that she shows them freely. The Captain has no more right to visit the Boy's bank for pennies because he is her brother, than she has to abstract money from the grocery-man's till. You have no more right to obtrude your conversation upon your wife, nor she upon her husband, when either is in the middle of a thrilling story, than you or she would have to interrupt the Queen of England at her devotions. An "excuse me," if a mother is obliged to interrupt her youngest child's babble, is quite as good a way to teach the baby manners as a course of lectures later on etiquette. The man who gets up and slams shut the ventilator in a crowded car to suit his own convenience, or the woman who throws open a car-window regardless of the occupants of the seat behind her, is no ruder than Bess is when she ignores brother Tom's comfort at home, or Tom is when he pounces for the biggest orange on the plate when only Bess and he are at table. When either makes rude remarks to the other, they sin against the true code of etiquette more than when they are discourteous at a party or boisterously unkind with a comrade, just as he is more criminally careless who pounds a piano to pieces with a hammer than he who batters the pine case it was brought in. The greater the value of the article, the choicer we are supposed to be of it, and in the same line of argument, the dearer and closer the tie that binds us, the more considerate we should be in the handling of it. I may hurt the feelings of a society acquaintance, and there is restitution and forgiveness, but when I stab the dear old mother's heart with an unkind word, or wound my child's feelings with an injustice or a cruelty, or ridicule the sensitive feelings of a brother or a sister, not eternity itself shall be long enough to extract the sting from my memory when my dear ones are dead and love's opportunity is vanished forever.

Study politeness, then, which is the body-guard of love, and build up for yourself the structure of a happy home.

Has it been borne in upon you what radiant mornings and September nights the last two weeks have brought in? Have you stopped, Mr. Busyman, to note the wonder of the skies, never so glorious as of late? Did you see the sunset the other evening when a gigantic cloud stood almost zenith high against the flaming west, and took on for a time the panoply of a king? Did you notice the purple center and the dazzling edge, with the rose blush that fringed its borders? Did you see it pale to gray and vanish like a ghost into the starry night? Do you ever stop, Mrs. Featherhead, to mark the beauty of our wayside clover or the sparkle of a buttercup in the dew? Have you found the nooks where, like shy children, the violets cluster? Did you mark a certain day, a week or so ago, when the heavens were full of cloud battalions, taking new shapes every minute, and often dissolving in long lines of purple rain, shot through with stitches of golden light? Have you seen the lake lately, as blue as a heather bell, as wild as a wood-bird, as peaceful as a brooding dove? Where were you the other night when out of the sullen storm cloud the "light that never was on land or sea" enfolded us, and the world hung like an emerald in a topaz sky?

No law of morals should be less arbitrary for men than it is for women. An impure heart, a riotous appetite, a profane tongue, are no more excusable in a man than they are in a woman. If a man is supposed to shrink from selecting his wife among the unclean in thought and immoral of practice, why should not a young girl be allowed an undefiled selection? When girls grow so queenly natured that they demand that their lover should be of the royal stock and never demean themselves to stoop to mate with impurity and profligacy just because it carries a handsome face and a well-filled pocketbook, there will be some chance for happiness in the married estate. It is this placing white flowers in smutty buttonholes, or, in other words, the wedding of pure women to blasé and wicked men, that sows the seed of the tare in what was meant by the primal law to be a harvest of golden grain. Do you pick slug-eaten roses and wind-fall blossoms? When you go forth to buy material for a new gown do you choose cotton warp fabrics and colors that will fade in the first washing? Your answers to all these question are prompt enough, but when I ask you what choice you make of gentlemen friends, you are not quite so ready with a reply. Do you choose the young man who has a clean record, who neither drinks nor wastes his money in riotous practices? How about the tobacco chewers and the swearers? How about the lewd jesters and the low-minded? Provided he wears fine clothes, can dance well and make a good appearance in society, and above all can give you a handsome diamond for an engagement ring, are you not willing to accept a lover in spite of his known reputation as a fast young man about town? Girls, you had much better choose a specked peach for canning than such a man for a husband. Do you imagine that by and by at the upper court, whither we are all hastening as quickly as the old patrol wagon of time can carry us, there will be any distinction made between men and women? Think you a man is going to get off easier than a sorrowful and sinful woman merely because the world falsely taught him that the exigencies of his nature demanded greater latitude than hers?

You may retouch a faded picture, you may patch up an old piano, you may mend a shattered vase, but you cannot make a plucked rose grow again; it will wither and die in spite of every effort to restore it to the stem from which it fell. And so with the heart from which a low desire in the guise of an alluring temptation has snatched the flower of innocence. That heart will fade into hopeless loss unless a greater love than yours or mine intervenes to save. An impure soul never started out impure from the first any more than a peach was decayed in the blossom. It is the small beginnings, dear girls, that lead up to the bitter endings. The impure book read on the sly, the questionable jest laughed at in secret, the talk indulged in with a schoolmate or a friend which you would be unwilling for "mother" to hear, the horrible card circulated under the desk or behind the teacher's back, those are the beginnings of an ending sadder than the blight of any desolation that storm or drought or frost can bring upon the blossoms. If I only could, how gladly I would dip my pen to-night in a light that should outshine the electric splendor of our streets and write a message against the dark background of the sky, to startle young girls into the realization of the danger that lurks in the first indulgence of thoughts and companionships that are not pure. Avoid all such as you would avoid the contagion of small-pox, and a thousand times more. Small-pox, at its worst, can only mar the body, but the friend who lends you bad books or tells you "smutty" stories proffers a contagion to your soul which all the fountains of all your tears can never cleanse away.

THIS BABY OF OURS.

There's not a blossom of beautiful May,
Silver of daisy, or daffodil gay,
Nor the rosy bloom of apple tree flowers,
Fair as the face of this baby of ours.

You could never find, on a bright June day,
A bit of fair sky so cheery and gay;
Nor the haze on the hills in noonday hours,
Blue as the eyes of this baby of ours.

There's not a murmur of wakening bird—
The clearest, sweetest, that ever was heard
In the tender hush of the dawn's still hours—
Soft as the laugh of this baby of ours.

There's no gossamer silk of tasseled corn,
Nor the flimsiest thread of the shy wood fern—
Not even the cobwebs spread over the flowers—
Fine as the hair of this baby of ours.

There's no fairy shell by the sounding sea,
No wild rose that nods on the windy lea,
No blush of the sun through April's showers,
Pink as the palm of this baby of ours.

Don't you get awfully tired of people who are always croaking? A frog in a big, damp, malarial pond is expected to make all the fuss he can in protest of his surroundings. But a man! Destined for a crown, and born that he may be educated for the court of a king! Placed in an emerald world with a hither side of opaline shadow, and a fine dust of diamonds to set it sparkling when winter days are flying; with ten million singing birds to make it musical, and twice ten million flowers to make it sweet; with countless stars to light it up with fiery splendor, and white, new moons to wrap it round with mystery; with other souls within it to love and make happy, and the hand of God to uphold it on its rushing way among the countless worlds that crowd its path: what right has a man to find fault with such a world?

When the woodtick shall gain a hearing, as he complains that the grand old century oak is unfit to shelter him, or the bluebird be hearkened to when he murmurs that the horizon is off color, and does not match his wings, then, I think, it will be time for man to find fault with the appointments of the magnificent sphere he inhabits.

"It is a fine day!" remarks Miss Cherry-lips.

"Too cold," says the croaker; "beastly wind, not fit for a dog to breathe."

Oh, yes, my dear, I heard him say it this very morning, and while I sat and listened to him I could but think to myself, "What would become of the croaker without the weather topic to fall back upon?" When all else failed him, he is sure to have something to find fault with within the range of this universal and inexhaustible topic. It is too warm or too cold; there is too much rain, or there is a drought; the winters are changing and microbes are on the increase; the peach buds are blighted by a cold snap in spring, and the potatoes have failed or are about to fail, owing to a wet June.

That is the way the croaker holds forth whenever he can get anybody to listen to him. I sometimes wonder what he would do if he really had great things to fret about; if one of his beautiful children were to die, or the faithful wife he loves so well in his heart, perhaps, but never takes the trouble to acquaint with the fact, were to weary of his endless faultfinding and steal away from it all into the quietude of the grave. I wonder if he would not then look back upon these days of "croaking" with amazement that he was ever so blind and stupid a fool.

I knew a woman once who was very, very charming. She could sing "Allan Percy" in a way that would melt the heart within you. She could paint on china and decorate the panels of doors, and on the whole she was calculated to enjoy life and make it enjoyable for others. But her home, on the contrary, was utterly devoid of peace and comfort. Her husband took no pleasure there, although he was lavish in the expenditure of money to render the place attractive. Her children were glad to get away from their home and find otherwhere the freedom and gaiety denied them there. Why was all this, when the mother was so eminently fitted by grace and accomplishments to create a beautiful and happy home? Simply because she was always fretting and fussing about trifles. She was a croaker and always finding fault. She fought flies until life was a burden to everybody who watched her. She said that they would spoil the paint, poison the food and ruin the curtains. She was after them at early dawn nor gave over the chase until late at night. She would leave the dinner table to chase a fly and kill it with a folded paper. She would stop the lullaby song she was singing to her pretty baby, to get up and call somebody to come in and hunt a stray blue-bottle that was bunting its stupid head against the window screen. She said that her life wasn't worth a farthing to her if the flies got into her home, and she would sooner jump in the river than submit to the pestilential infliction. Then she was forever prophesying some dreadful fate for herself by reason of the muddy footprints that occasionally found their way onto the carpets.

"I declare," she would say, "if you boys don't stop tracking dirt into the house I'll die before my time. If there is anything I hate it is a careless boy!"

And the boys took her at her word and stopped tracking mud. But they were gradually lured to stay away from home, and the soil they took into their hearts was perhaps harder to efface than the footmarks they left upon the floor of mother's neatly kept hallways.

She was always anticipating trouble that never came. She knew the girl was going to leave. She was simply too great a treasure to keep. She was absolutely certain that the milkman was watering his milk, and the baby would get sick. She had no doubt whatever but what her husband was going to ruin himself on 'Change, and then what would become of them all? So she worried and fretted and fumed, until patience, like a hunted bird, spread its wings and flew away, and what might have been a happy home became a stranded wreck upon the rocks of contention.

Oh, I tell you right now, girls, if you can only cultivate one accomplishment out of the many that wait to crown a perfect womanhood, cultivate a pleasant temper and cheerful disposition. The ability to speak many languages, to paint, to dance, to sing, or even to wield a graceful pen is nothing compared to the ability to make a lovely home. Nobody ever yet succeeded in that noblest endeavor without abjuring needless faultfinding, croaking and fretting.

As a general thing I don't believe in sermons served as restaurants serve beef—in slices. I believe in teaching truths, rather, as one whips cream, dropping in the moral as an almost imperceptible flavoring. But I tell you there are times when I feel like mounting a pulpit and thundering with old Calvin, until the air emits sulphur. Especially when I see the inhumanities and outrages practiced upon children by witless parents, do I feel stirred to my soul's depths. If we treated our flower beds as we do our children there wouldn't be a blossom left in the world. If we served our meals as we do our children, there would be rampant indigestion and black-browed death at the heels of every one of us. Now and then you see a wise mother and sensible father, but the biggest half of humanity receive their children as youngsters receive their Christmas toys, to be played with when in a good humor, and bundled anywhere out of sight when out of sorts or engrossed with more important matters. We forget, half of us, that a little child's sense of injustice and sorrow and wrong is compatible with its own growth and experience rather than with our own. What to us is a paltry trial is the cause of keenest, unalleviated woe to the child of five. The possession of uncounted gold at forty will not be more precious than the possession at three of the apple or the book we so rudely snatch from the little hands without a word of apology. Take the time to explain to the little fellow why you deprive him of some cherished possession and you will save the tender bit of a heart a vast amount of unnecessary aching.

I have many things to be thankful for this stormy winter night. One is that the coal bin is full and the lock on the outer door secure. Another is that the rooftree bends above an unbroken band, and that disease with its fell touch lingers the other side of the threshold of the little home. Another is that, as a family, we all have straight backs and moderately developed intellects; that we are neither dime museum freaks, lunatics, nor half-wits. Another is that none of us chew gum, carry around dogs, nor make expectoration the chief business of a day's outing. Another is that I am getting so used to the alarm clock that I sleep through its wild clamor and escape the duties that fall to the lot of that other member of the home circle whose ear and conscience are not so sadly seared as mine. Another is that I know enough to detect butter from oleomargarine, and am not roped in by

Blank street vendors with their dollar and a half tubs. Another is that I am not the sort of fellow to be always hitting another fellow when he has been down and is trying to stand steady again. Another is that I am modest enough to question whether I could run a grip any better than he does? Another is that I got one answer to the "ad." wherewith I sought to capture a gold watch. It would have been an embarrassing thing to have received not one solitary little nibble. Another is that the elevator boy who occasionally carries me to the top floor and intermediate stations around at Blank's is kind and does not treat me with the haughty scorn he bestows on others. Another is that I have the serene equipoise of nerve which renders me calm and even cheerful under the knowledge that there is nothing in the house to eat, and two invited guests gently sleeping the happy hours away in the chamber above, dreaming perchance of toothsome viands not to be. Another is that in spite of weather I take no colds, and am as impervious to catarrhal or pneumonic affections as an eagle is impervious to the attack of tom-tits. Another is that I live in a town where people sell no beer; they may steal and backbite, and raise the old lad generally, but thank goodness the baleful glitter of a glass beer bottle has never yet eclipsed the moral splendor of the scene. Another is that I have been enabled to preserve a few staunch and trusty friends through the evolution of that rainy-weather costume which a few of my sex have joined me in essaying. I cannot speak for future tests, but so far my henchmen have stood firm. And right here let me say that any friend, man, woman or babe, who can remain loyal to you after you have been seen in public in a dress-reform garment is worth cultivating, and should be made the theme of special psalms of praise. Another is that the picture I had taken the other day looks worse than I do, and when I send it off to unsuspecting admirers I am not torn with the thought that when they see the original they will drop scalding hot tears of disappointment. This idea of raising false hopes in the minds of confiding strangers savors too much of Ananias and Sapphira. Another is that so far in life I have preserved a stern and unshaken resolution not to wear a false front. A woman in a store bang is next worse to a chromo in an art gallery, or a muslin rose among American beauties fresh from the rose gardens. Artificiality, my dear, pretense and assumption, are harder to put up with than anything else in the world, unless it is corns. But far ahead of all the above enumerated causes for gratitude is one which thrills me most profoundly, and which can be summed up in half a dozen words, the echo of which, perhaps, will find a lodgment in some other hearts. I am thankful, very, very thankful, that I am not the mother, nor the aunt, nor the half-sister, nor the first cousin, nor even the next-door neighbor, of the boy who kills sparrows for two cents bounty on the little heads. If I had such a boy within range of my voice to-night I should say to him, "Be poor, my man; be unsuccessful in business, and not up to bargains all your life, but don't be shrewd and sordid and cruel in seeking your gains. Better go by the name of 'mollycoddle' and 'baby' among the other boys than get to be a little ruffian with your arrow and your sling-shot, and the name of a keen-killer tacked on to yourself. Let the sparrows alone, or if you really feel that they are the nuisance they are made out to be, kill them if you like, but do it in a gentlemanly way (if such a paradox is possible), and don't take money for the job." The boy or the man who will take a life for sordid ends, or, in other words, who will seek to enrich himself on "blood money," is pretty low down in the human scale.

Laughter is a positive sweetness of life, but, like good coffee, it should be well cleared of deleterious substance before use. Ill-will and malice and the desire to wound are worse than chicory. Between a laugh and a giggle there is the width of the horizons. I could sit all day and listen to the hearty and heartsome ha! ha! of a lot of bright and jolly people, but would rather be shot by a Winchester rifle at short range than be forced to stay within earshot of a couple of silly gossips. Cultivate that part of your nature that is quick to see the mirthful side of things, so shall you be enabled to shed many of life's troubles, as the plumage of the bird sheds rain. But discourage all tendencies to seek your amusement at the expense of another's feelings or in aught that is impure. It was Goethe who said:

"Tell me what a man laughs at and I will read you his character."

I'll take my chances any day to find heaven on earth, if I can have the run of the woods up along our northern lake shore in early springtime. I want no companions either, unless, perhaps, it be a child or a dog, for artificial women and dudish men, let loose in the woods, are harder to endure than gad-flies. It was scarcely more than sunrise, the other morning, when I left the house and took my way toward the forest shrine undesecrated as yet by surveyors or wood-choppers, the advent of either of whom in a country town means good-bye to heaven on that particular spot of earth! We found the air so full of sweetness, the instant we struck the depths of the woods, that one could almost fancy the wise men of the East had been there before us to greet the new-born Spring with spices as they greeted another Heaven-born child a score of centuries ago in Bethlehem. Every shrub held a softly-tinted leafbud half unfolded, like a listless hand. The maple leaves were pink and glossy, like rose petals wet with rain. The hickory trees were unfolding great creamy buds that looked like magnolias. The hawthorns were all afloat with silver blossoms, like loosened sails. The earth seemed singing to the heavens, "God is here!" and from the blue depths of quietude, where a few clouds spread their soft wings like brooding birds, came back the answer, "He is here!" The lake claimed Him, and a thousand azure waves murmured His presence on the deep. Wherever we looked, at our feet where the June lilies whitened the ground like perfumed snow, and the moss was bubbling like a wayside spring with sunshine in place of water; at the misty foliage overhead, like shadowy spirit wings; at the circle of blue that bounded the earth, or into the very heart of heaven above us, it seemed as though God, visible and manifest, was there to give us greeting. Finally, we found a point of high land, touched here and there with shadows flung down from budding birches, and starred with dandelions in flocks, like golden butterflies. Here, leaving the material part of me leaning up against a tree-trunk to rest, as one thrusts a cumbersome garment on a nail, my soul went wandering off into Paradise, and forgot awhile its environment and its earth-born responsibilities. Next time the world has failed to use you well and you are smarting from the sense of injury undeserved, or the frets of domestic life have worn you down to the minimum, like a blade that is eternally upon the grindstone, start for the woods. Take a big basket with you and fill it full of lilies, and, ten to one, before you get home again the lilies will have taken root in your heart and your basket will be full of contentment.

Educate the children to the expectation of sorrow, not as a monster who is to devour them, but as an angel who is to meet them on the way and lead them gently home to heaven. Teach them to hold themselves in readiness for whatever life has in store, as soldiers are trained for a battle whose end is certain peace. Teach them to endure all things, only striving to sweeten and soften rather than to harden under the discipline of sorrow. Unselfishness is the most rare and at the same time the most Christian virtue possible for human nature to attain to, but did anybody ever yet grow unselfish through a life of indolent self-indulgence and ease? Did fruit ever amount to anything that was left unacquainted with the sharp discipline of the gardener's shears? I tell you, all the way up from an apple to a man it takes lots of pruning and lopping off of superfluous branches to bring out the flavors and sweeten the fiber of the fruit.

I can imagine a lot of way-worn pilgrims drawing up to heaven's gate.

"What will you have?" asks old St. Peter, standing idle and calm in the perpetual sunshine that lies beyond the swinging portal.

"I will have my crown," says one. "I have earned it."

"And I will have my harp," says another; "my fingers are eager to pick out the heavenly tunes."

"And I will hie me at once to my heavenly mansion," says a third. "Long time I have plodded, foot-sore and weary, to gain the habitation of its enduring rest."

But if you can imagine "Amber" piping forth her small request, I think you might hear her say: "Conduct me, oh, aged friend, to the nearest sand-bank, where I may lie face downward in the sunshine for fifty years to come, and hear the surf break on 'Sconsett's reef." That is what I have been doing for the past fortnight, and both soul and body have waxed strong in the process.

What a tired passenger we carry around with us, sometimes, in this marvelous Pullman coach of ours, wherein the soul takes passage for its overland trip from the cradle to the grave. How restless it gets, and how troublesome. How it turns from companionship, even that of books, and finds no panacea for its torment, until some kind fate side-tracks it and lets the noisy world rumble on with the clatter and clash of conflicting cares beating the hours to dust beneath their flying wheels.

When I went away for my yearly outing I was so cross that there was no living within six miles of my own shadow. I hated everything on earth, and everything on earth hated me. But I have come back as sweetly as the breath of a rose steals through a lattice. That is the effect of a jaunt, my dear; and let me say right now that if you are holding on to your money in the hope of getting rich sometime, or if you are traveling in a rut because you think you are too poor to avoid it, or if you are grinding your soul into fine dust in the process of laying up against a rainy day, just stop right where you are and listen to me. Any money that is gained at the expense of health, either physical or mental; any duty held to in the face of nervous breakdown; any gain secured at the expense of peace of mind and growth of soul, is not worth the holding. You cannot be of any use in the world if you are worn out or sick. You may persist in holding on, but your grip is weak, and your effect on affairs and people is simply that of an irritant. You owe it to yourself, as well as to others, to go away and get rested. If it costs money to do so, consider money well spent that gains so fair an equivalent as rest and change, and renewed vigor. I tell you there are few better uses to which you may put your dollars than in a yearly outing. Your pockets may be lighter when you get back, but so will your heart be, and the few sacrifices necessary in the way of less expensive clothes and cigars, or less frequent gloves and bonnets, will be well worth the making for the result gained.

I wish Columbus had never discovered us. I wish that he had never steered his old bark westward and found the "land of the free and the home of the brave." For with discovery came civilization, and I believe we would have been better off without it. If we only could have been left to ourselves and gone on sitting under lotus trees unaffected by dressmaker and tailor bills, I believe the sum total of happiness would have been far greater in the world than it is to-day. I would love to return to my allegiance to nature and forever desert the haunts of civilization and the marts of trade. I want to gather together a picked band of kindred souls and go out and pitch tent by the Gunnison River. Ever been there? Imagine a stream of gold flowing through hills colored like an apple orchard in May, with a sky bending down above them like the wing of an oriole. I want to forget the insolence of a class who may be as good as I am in the eye of the law, but whom it would take a ton of soap and God's grace to make my equal in point of cleanliness and decency. I want to forget forever the clang of the cable car and the rumble of its wheels. I want to return to the heathendom that worships gods instead of dollars and loves mankind simply because it knows nothing of faithlessness and fraud.

"Plaze, sor," said a servant to the head of a certain suburban household the other morning, "the gintleman who stuole the chickens left his hat in the hincoop." Just so, Bridget. And the lady who attends to the affairs of the kitchen has her foot upon the neck of the miserable woman who is nominally at the head of the house. Oh, no! I am not going to enter into a disquisition upon the merits of the servant question. Years ago, when I cantered lightly in my ride against windmills, I might have undertaken it, but the question has grown too large to be settled by talking. The state of things in this free country is growing just a trifle too free. There are no longer any servants in this proud land. It is not ladylike to serve. The person who superintends the domestic affairs of our home merely condescends for a consideration. We no longer have any rights as employers. The wind has tacked to another quarter. Should we wish to discharge our lady cook or dispense with the services of a gentleman artisan it stands in place for us to approach them in a respectful manner, put the case before them clearly and ask them humbly, without offense to their delicate sensibilities, if they will kindly allow us to forego their so-called services. Question yourself seriously, my dear; are you sufficiently considerate? Think how these defenseless ladies and thin-skinned gentlemen who fill positions of trust in your establishment must suffer sometimes from your boorish impetuosity. Are you always cordial in your greeting when the worn face of the cook appears at the delayed breakfast hour and she places before you the hurried pancake and the underdone steak? Do you stop to think how the poor creature has danced all night at a ball and has crept home after your stiff-necked and rebellious husband has bounded away to catch the early train, breakfastless and profane? And when the low-voiced and timid second girl tells you that, as a lady who knows her place, she really cannot demean herself to wipe off the paint or sweep the front steps, do you take her by the hand and acknowledge the indiscretion of your coarser nature in expecting her to do such menial service? How many of us, clods that we are, have raged when the mild-mannered laundry maid has appropriated our underclothing, or remonstrated when the number seven foot of the blue-blooded cook has condescended to stretch our silken hose? It behooves us to join the ranks of the "philanthropic fiends" and look to it that we improve our methods of treating the delicate gentry who tarry with us so briefly.

By the way, I think I occasionally hear a feeble pipe from a man to the effect that the girls are responsible for all the tomfoolery in the world. Don't you know that you are the very ones who tend to make them so— you men? You follow after and woo and wed just that sort of girls. You won't look at a sensible little woman who can make "lovely" bread, abjures bangs, can't dance and has no "style." You laugh at and make sly jokes at the expense of our big hats and our pronounced fashions, but when you choose your company, and often your wives, I notice you pass right by the home-keeping birds and take the peacocks. Of course, no one lives in this age who doubts for a moment that woman's chief aim in life and purpose of creation, as well as her hope of a blessed hereafter, is to please the men and get a husband. If you won't have her modest and simply gowned she is willing to make a feather-headed doll and a travesty of herself to get you and win heaven! You know perfectly well, you men, that you don't care half so much for brains as you do for general "get-up," and the woman you honor with your choice is selected for a pretty face and form, and a becoming costume rather than for a clever head and an honest heart. I am not talking to old fogies who cling to old-fashioned notions, but to young men who ridicule the customs of their grandmothers, who shake their heads at salaries of two and three thousand a year as inadequate to support wives; who rail against woman's extravagance, yet do their best to maintain her in it. When you, my fine and dapper gentleman, begin to seek out the modestly appareled and the sedate girls, then shall folly and vain show fly over seas for want of encouragement and the grand transformation of sawdust dolls into women and pleasure-seekers into home-keepers take place.

TWO DAYS.

I said to myself one golden day
When the world was bright and the world was
    gay,
  "Though I live more lives than time has years
  Either in this or the infinite spheres,
I will fear no blight and I'll bear no cross,
Against my gains I will write no loss,
  But I and my soul, twin lilies together,
  Shall whiten in endless summer weather!"

I said to myself one weary day
When the world was old and the world was gray,
  "Has God forgotten His wandering earth?
  Are its tears His scorning, its groans His
    mirth?
There's no blue above where the torn clouds fly,
There's no bloom below where the dead leaves
    lie;
  Would I and my soul were at rest together
  Wrapped from the chill of this wintry
    weather."

There are some people who live in this world as a cucumber grows in a garden. They cling to their own vine and serve no higher end than rotundity and relish. There are others who live in the world as a summer breeze lives in a meadow; they find out all the hidden flowers and set the perfumes flying. There are others who live as the sea lives in a shell; their existence is nothing but a sigh. There are others who live as the fire lives in a diamond; they are all sparkle. And there are others, and they outnumber all the rest, who live as a blind mole lives in the soil; they see nothing, feel nothing, suffer and enjoy a little now and then, perhaps, but know nothing to all eternity. Such people walk through life as the mole walks through the glory of a summer day, or burrows beneath the dazzle of a winter storm. They are as irresponsive to the voices all about them as the mole is to the singing of April robins. They are as untouched by the myriad influences of life as the mole is by the light of a star or the flash of a comet. Their only interest is in the question, "Wherewith shall we be clothed, and what shall we have to eat?" They gather the ripened hours from the tree of life as a child gathers fruit, merely for the gratification of an instant appetite, not as the careful housewife does, who garners in a store for wintry weather. Life to them is merely a fattening process. They remind one of prize beef at a county fair; to-morrow brings the shambles and the butcher's axe, but in the serene content of a well-filled stall and a full stomach, they take no thought of the future. We meet such people every day and everywhere. On the streets they may see a brute tyrannizing over a helpless beast of burden, or a mother (?) yanking a sobbing child along by the arm, as full of ugliness herself as a thunder-cloud is of electricity, or a man following an innocent young girl with the devil in his heart, or a big boy tyrannizing over a smaller one; and they pass it all by as indifferently as the mole would sneak across a battlefield the morning after a battle. They have too much to do themselves to waste time in remedying other people's grievances. They think too much of personal reputation to involve themselves in an altercation with defilers of the innocent, and tramplers of the weak. They are too respectable to get mixed up in brawls, even if the disturbance is brought about by the devil's own drummers looking up recruits among the championless and defenseless working-girls, or the parentless and homeless children of a great city. We meet them traveling through the mountains or loitering by the sea. Their only use for mountains is that they may carve their precious initials on the highest peaks, pick winter-greens and blue-berries and display their fashionable suits and striped stockings. They look upon the sea as a big bathing-tank, and the sky, with all its splendor of cloud and its glory of sunrise and sunset, as a barometer to forecast the weather. We meet them in business relations, and they never believe that courtesy and business can go together. A merchant in his office or a lady in her parlor will bluntly refuse to buy of a worn-out, discouraged, heart-sick book-agent, ignoring the fact that a smile accompanying even a refusal acts like a spoonful of sugar in bitter tea, and costs less. Even a "lady" clerk, behind a counter, will be haughty and unaccommodating and insolent to the woman who comes to buy, forgetful that a customer will go a long distance out of her way to deal with a polite and well-mannered clerk, and that, like honesty, politeness is ever the best policy. And, on the other hand, a woman shopper will be whimsical and captious and trying, forgetting that the girl who serves her has human blood in her veins, and often carries a troubled heart behind her smile or her frown.

They have come! Without the sound of a bugle, the bright hosts have marched down and taken possession of the land. The southern slopes are all alive with their wind-shaken tents, and when the sun comes out warm and glowing from the cloudy pavilions of the April sky, he finds a million blossoms on the hills that yesterday were white with snow. Some of them are tinted like the flush that lingers in the evening sky before the stars find it; some of them are stainless as unfallen snow; some of them are purple as a nautillus sail adrift upon a twilight sea; and all of them are joyfully welcome to hearts that are weary of Winter's long reign. And after the hypatica shall come the violet, and after the violet the trillium, and after the trillium the wild-rose, and after the wild-rose the cardinal-flower and the wood-lily, and after them the gentian and the golden rod, to mark the wane of the year. Oh, who would not live in a world whose dial-plate is made of flowers and whose circling seasons are told over with blossoming trees and gentian-buds?

I saw a great many things on the way this morning as I was coming to town. Suppose, as the weather is too warm for preaching, I enumerate them and let you strike the balance at the close, to see which way the world is jogging. I saw a father, drunk, beside his little blue-eyed daughter. His head was laid in maudlin sleep upon her shoulder, and with blushes that came and went across her face like cloud shadows on the slope of a hill, she sat and bore the burden of her childish shame like a little angel. I saw a hard-faced, labor-grimed man step out of his way to pick a wild rose that grew by the side of the road. I saw a young man lash his horse because his own bungling driving came near colliding his vehicle with a cable car. I saw a policeman spring to the rescue of an old beggar woman who stumbled on a street crossing, and saw him fall and trampled upon in the discharge of duty. I saw a pretty girl reach out her white fingers and feed a discouraged street-car horse the banana she was eating as she passed by. I saw a beaten dog turn and fawn beneath his master's brutal kick, and I thought to myself, where is a more faithful friendship than that? I saw a little golden-headed boy at the window of a house as I rode by, and when I waved my hand he kissed his in return. I saw a tired mother stoop to hug the child who fidgeted at her knee in the tedious depot waiting-room, and I saw another slap her baby because its sticky fingers sought to fondle her cheek. I saw a little girl get up, without suggestion from her mother, and yield her seat to an older person. I saw a lamed and dying bird just brought down by a boy's sling-shot. (I saw that same boy in Sabbath-school last Sunday!) I saw one woman in fifty thousand wearing the dress-reform. I saw eleven girls out of nineteen with tightly-laced waists! I saw a hurt kitten tenderly attended to by a soldier in blue, as I passed Fort Sheridan Camp, and involuntarily I said to myself: "The bravest are the tenderest; the loving are the daring." I saw a small boy beating his mother with both fists because she carried him over the crowded and dangerous way, and so, I thought, we treat the tender God who sometimes lifts us, against our will, from evil ways. I saw a little coffin in an undertaker's window, and thought, what child in this busy, bustling city is doomed to fill that casket? What love-watched home shelters the head that shall one day sleep upon that satin pillow? I saw a teacher in one of our public schools and overheard a gross bit of slang as she passed by. I see myself sending a child of mine to such a teacher if I knew it! I saw a father wheeling his baby in a perambulator, with the sun blazing straight into its blinking eyes. I saw one man out of every ten dodge into a liquor saloon when he thought nobody was looking. I saw a homely girl transformed into a beauty by a service of love accorded a stranger. I saw a woman lean out of a Marshall Field 'bus to laugh at another who wore shabby clothes and walked with a drooping head. I saw lots of things besides, but how does the balance strike?

If we have been living on bad terms with a neighbor; if we have been maintaining a chilling silence and a forbidding reserve with anybody thrown often in our way, let us have done with such nonsense and live in the world as God meant we should.

Out of the exuberance of a merry heart the housekeeper has loosened the tacks in the parlor carpet, and the epoch of housecleaning begins. The head of the family, pro tem. dweller in the land of desolation and sojourner in the valley of wrath, hies him to town and wishes vainly for the return of the days when he had no wife save in Spain and no family outside of Elia's land of dreams. The calciminer comes and drops leprous splashes all over the hallways and the bannisters. One paperhanger taketh unto himself another, and the two scatter ringlets of snipped paper all over the bed chambers, and cumber up the floors with sticky paste-pots and brushes. The scrub woman breathes hard and devastates the approaches of the front steps, while the hired girl skips playfully here and there with damp cloths and bars of silvery soap. There is no breakfast, no lunch, no dinner. We take what provender the gods deliver to us in out of the way places, like stalled oxen or uncomplaining army mules! We sleep by night in beds loosely put together and smelling of soap. We awake betimes to the rattle of the scrubbing brush and the sharp overthrow of stovepipes. We see the young person, like McStinger, on the rampage from morn till night. We watch her hand to hand encounters with the pictures that have been wont to hang upon the walls. How she swoops upon them, bears them down, buffets them with dusters and heaps them high like stumbling blocks in the path of the righteous! How she sneers at our feeble, yet apt, suggestion, and pharisaically "thanks goodness that she is good for something besides standing around and giving unsolicited advice!" How she charges upon our cherished books and whacks them together vindictively to loosen the dust and the bindings! How she tosses the piano like a feather in her strength and probes its sensitive heart-strings with a knitting needle in search of dirt and pins! How she rebukes the Captain for idling away her time at doll-playing while there is so much work to do, and drives that gallant young field officer forth to do battle with the unresisting tomato can in the backyard! What a pandemonium reigns over all the domain of yesterday's content! Carlo, the dog, whose flippant youth is getting its first severe taste of life's discipline, retires to an adjacent covert and howls a fitful protest. The cat blinks sleepily in the sunshine and dreams of a future unmarred by suds and a slippery foothold. When she has occasion to walk across the kitchen floor she shakes her hind foot gingerly, like a pilgrim delicately removing the dust of the enemy's land from his members. The goblin brood of chickens chuckle with amazement while the hired man beats the rugs like a snare drum and charges upon the carpet that hangs like a vanquished foe across the clothesline. But, like everything else, my dear, we take the trials of spring housecleaning as the tourist takes the storms in the Alps or the sailor meets the tempest on the sea. It has not come to stay; the sun-lighted peaks of deliverance lie just ahead of us, and there is fine sailing for another year when the squall is weathered.

I am tired of the endless dress parade of the great alike—aren't you? I am tired of walking in file, as convicts walk together in stripes—aren't you? I glory in cranks who have enough individuality to refuse to be sewed up in the universal patchwork, like the calico blocks we used to overcast with our poor little pricked fingers ever so long ago when we were children—don't you? The onward sweep of progress in this age has prepared the way for non-conformists, and, glory be to God! they are swinging into line like beacon lights up the Maine coast. I confess I have no heart-pining for emancipation that shall place me alongside of Dr. Mary Walker or others of her ilk. I would like to retain my womanliness, but I would like also to make a distinct mark upon my times, be it ever so small and insignificant, as an individual and an intelligence quite as distinct from the conventional masses as a blackbird is when it leaves the flock and silhouettes itself in solitary state against the deep blue sky from the top of a windy elm tree—wouldn't you?

I want one good square fling on earth before I die. I want the chance to know what it is to have enough money to be able to buy silk elastic occasionally instead of cotton, and to have my teeth filled with gold instead of concrete without feeling as though I had been robbing hen-roosts for a month after. I want to go to the theater in a swell carriage, and sit in the best box, with a pale pink ostrich boa draped about my shoulders and the opera-glasses of the entire house leveled at me for a stunning beauty. I want the sensation, for once, of knowing that I am as handsome as I am bright, and as well-dressed as I am virtuous. I want to have ice cream seven times a week and "Pommery Sec" by the dozen in the cellar. I want to own a silk umbrella with a golden crook, and wear a diamond ring on every finger. I want to buy candy whenever I feel like it without having to register it in the family account book under the head of "sundries" and "cough drops." I want to see the time when I can call the average shop-girl out into the alley and have it out with her with none to interfere. I want to settle with her for the indignities I have long suffered with the pusillanimity of a meek nature. I want to ask her between clips why she has always sold me just what I didn't want, and sneered at me because I didn't buy more of it. I want also to engage in hand to hand conflict with the female gum-chewer. I want to convince her that I have endured all I will of her facial contortions, and that the time has come for the extinction of her type from the face of the blooming earth. I want the power to consign every man who even mentions "nose bag" to a horse, to the guillotine, and to imprison for life every brute who carries a snake-whip or uses a check-rein. I want to solder the man or woman who objects to fresh air inside a tin can and label them "sardines." I want to shoot on sight the first human being who mentions the word "draught" in my hearing, and set my dog on the fiend who blots the face of nature with his ear-muffs. I want to live for a while in a country where there are neither thunderstorms nor cyclones, but where I can sleep nights right through, from March until November, without getting up to look for funnels or shooing the whole family down cellar as a hen gathers her chickens from the swooping hawk. I want to live in a community made up of people who mind their own business. I want to be able now and then to receive a letter from out of town (it is generally a bill!) without having the village postmaster regard me as a burning fagot. I want to find a recipe for making buckwheat cakes that do not taste like sand. I want to be able to detect a hypocrite and a traitor on sight, without waiting for a broken heart to evidence the fact that I am sold again. I want to rise out of the range of small annoyances, and fly above the aim of inferior people to disturb. I want to grow to be more like an eagle that wings its way out of the habitat of gadflies, and less like a trembling hare pursued by hounds. I want to take the lesson to my heart that the soul that is constant to itself and aspires towards heaven shall never be left a prey to care and unrest. I want to strike a dress reform which shall make women look less like guys, and to encounter a rainy day in which I shall not bite the dust, I and my umbrella, and my flippety-floppety skirts, and my nineteen bundles. I want to cut down the ballot privilege and make it impossible for an immigrant to vote before he is a twenty-one-year resident of America. I want to convince the woman suffragist that the greatest curse she can precipitate upon her sex is the ballot. I want to teach my sisters that if they will pay more attention to their homes and less to outside issues American institutions will be more of a success. If the career of a politician will spoil a man what would it do for a woman? On the principle that a strawberry will decay sooner than a pumpkin, or that a violet is more fragile than a sunflower, it would take about one election day to change a woman into a harridan. I never knew but one out and out politician who preserved intact the amenities of a gentleman, and he died early of heart trouble. The thing killed him physically before it destroyed him morally. If any politician reads this and wants to challenge the point I want to meet him and either convince him or be slain.

If you are not glad to be alive such weather as this it is because you are a clod and not

a sentient being. Why, I never open my
door these radiant mornings and walk out
into a world that is more golden than any
topaz and more radiant than any diamond
that I do not hug myself for very joy that I
am alive! The grave has not got me yet!
And, though I be poor and quite alone and
go hungry for the fleshpots that make my
neighbors great about the girth, I am happy
as a queen and quite content to cast my lot
with clovers and birds and wayside weeds
that feel the vigor of summer weather in
every fiber of prodigal life. To-night the
sky was like the flame of King Solomon's
opal—did you see it? And just as the glory
was growing and deepening into an intensity of beauty that made you want to shut
your eyes and say Oh—h—h! as the little
boys do at the circus when the elephants go
round, a thrush whipped out his mellow flute
and gave us a vesper song that made one
think of heaven and bands of singing angels!
And yet we are discontented and feel ourselves misused because we happen to be a
little poverty-stricken now and then, and it
is hard work to find the plums in our pudding!

The other morning, before the town clock struck 7, I was riding over country in a hack, driven by a courtly mannered colored boy and drawn by a couple of discouraged mules. I was going over to Hampton and Chesapeake City to see the sights. A robin was quarreling with a sparrow for possession of a nest in a treetop hung with blossoms thick as Monday's washing, and a small pickaninny stood in a doorway and held his breath with terror as our driver slashed the air with his long whip. The morning was superb. The sea lay like an opal with a dark setting of hills shadowed like oxidized silver, the birds were out like blossoms of the upper air with song in place of perfume, and the world seemed altogether too jolly and bright a spot to link with thoughts of sorrow and pain and death. We drove over to the soldiers' home, where from four to five thousand veteran warriors have found shelter from the bombarding storm of mundane care. Under the shadow of great willows in half-leaf and still golden with April sap, in sunny corners of broad piazzas, on benches by the slope of sluggish streams, or walking about the well-kept paths, these old and battle-scarred warriors pass the time away.

"What a hero I might have been," says each one to himself, "if only ——!" or, "What a narrow miss I made of glory when that premature shell took off my legs and stranded me here!" Peacefully they behold life's sun decline, and peacefully in turn they take possession of the narrow beds awaiting them in the near cemetery, where so many soldiers are sleeping the unheeded years away. Without motive or purpose their life is scarcely more eventless than their death shall finally be. Some way the grounds where these patient old graybeards sit day after day with nothing to do but muse upon the past remind me of the human heart with its pensioned hopes, its stranded intentions and its crippled endeavors! What heroisms, what subtle intents for good, what pretentious desires were frustrated and made worthless by the destiny which changed life's battlefield into a "soldiers' home" and the scene of action for the shaded seat under the willows of a long regret!

I wonder if Eve, looking over the battlements of heaven now and then, and seeing how tired we get down here and how discouraged and broken-hearted we often are, is ever sorry for the heritage she left us, all for the sake of an apple! Does she not curse the memory of the earth fruit whose flavor has so embittered humanity! Think of it, oh far-removed and perverse ancestress, if it were not for you we might have lived in a world where dinners walked into the pot and boiled themselves over fires that called for no replenishing; where rent stockings lifted themselves on viewless hands and were deftly darned by sunshine needles in the air; where last year's garments glided into this year's styles without the snip of scissors or the whirr of sewing machine wheels; where brooms swept and dust-cloths dusted unassisted by human hands; where windows cleaned themselves as fogs lift from the lake, and washing and ironing were spontaneous, like the growth of flowers. I for one am heartily tired of having to suffer for Eve's heartless stupidity. Hard work has too much of the blight of the primal curse about it to suit me, and no matter what philosophy we call to our aid the fact remains that labor of a certain sort is the heritage of sin, and sin was, is and ever shall be accursed.

But there is something a great deal worse than hard work, and that is laziness. The man who toils until the great muscles of his arm stand out like cords and his broad shoulders are bent like the branches of a pine under the force of a strong wind from the north is a king among his kind compared to the shiftless do-nothings of life, between whose feet are spun the cobwebs of sloth and within whose lily-white fingers nothing more burdensome than a cigar finds its way. Give me a blacksmith any day rather than a dude. Work is hard and sometimes thankless, but, like tough venison served with jelly sauce, it is spiced with self-respect and smacks of honest independence.

THE STORY OF A ROSE.

A white rose grew in a garden place,
On a slender stem, with a royal grace;
The nursling of June and her gentle showers,
Fairest and sweetest of all her flowers.

The south wind was out one day for a sail,
In a cloudy boat, so fleecy and frail,
And he chanced to spy, where musing she stood,
My dear little rose in her snowy hood.

Rosemary and Rue.

Oh, softly he whispered and tenderly sighed,
"Starry Eyes, Starry Eyes, I wait for my bride."
But she laughed in his face, and told him to go;
She didn't see why he bothered her so.

A dewdrop fell in the starry hush,
Lured from heaven by her dreamy blush;
But the tender kiss of his balmy lip
She gave to a bee, next morning, to sip.

A bobolink left the bloom of a tree
To tell her tale of whimsical glee;
The moon dropped a pearl to wear in her breast;
Dawn wove her a cloak of silvery mist.

But her hard little heart was colder than ice,
She sent every suitor away in a trice;
Till the wind drew nigh, with a terrible roar,
And said: "Pretty Rose, your playtime is o'er."

He shook her with might, and he drenched her with rain,
Till the poor little rose swooned away with her pain;
And her shiny crown, with its moonbeam glow,
He tossed far and wide, like the feathery snow.

And all that is left of that splendid bloom,
The diadem gay, and the spicy perfume,
Is a handful of dust, that once was a rose—
The sport of the wind, as it fitfully blows.

Rosemary and Rue.

Once upon a time there lived a woman. She was not very young, nor was she very old. She was neither handsome, homely, a genius, nor a fool. She was just a commonplace, good-intentioned, fair type of the average woman. This woman prided herself but little upon the various accomplishments that contribute to the modern woman's popularity. She could not dance a step, save in front of a northeast gale, or in a game of romps with her little folks. She could not decorate a tea cup to save her life, nor hand-paint a clam shell, nor embellish a canvas with fleshy cupids and no less corpulent rosebuds. She could sing a few insignificant ballads, such as "Annie Laurie," "Twilight Dews," and "Nearer, My God, to Thee." These with a number like them, she was always ready to furnish in a manner to bring down the house, but I doubt if she would have been a success either in a comic opera or a church choir. She could make bread and pieplant pie after a fashion that would make a man wish that he had been born earlier to enjoy more of them. She could tidy up a room quicker than a cat could wink its eyes, and in the matter of housecleaning she was a regular four-in-hand coach and a tiger. If you had asked her to lead a class in ethical culture or make a speech on suffrage or score a point for reform, this woman would have ignobly turned her back and run away, and yet perhaps she wielded an influence in the world quite as strong as many a woman whose name is recorded on the roll call of noisy fame. But there was one thing this woman abhorred with all the might and strength of her soul, and that was slang. She had been brought up to consider the use of anything more pronounced than the "yea" and "nay" of the Quaker vernacular an outrage to refinement, and although drifting far from her childhood's faith in many ways still preserved an innate shrinking from the exuberance of vain speech. She allowed no little boys to slide the cellar door with her own precious yellow-heads who could be positively convicted of using naughty language. Her husband left his worldly ways in town and only carried home to this nice little woman the aroma of propriety and coriander seeds. But who ever yet was assured of a firm foothold upon the pinnacle of self-righteousness that the old boy did not whip out an arrow and bring them low? It becomes my painful duty to chronicle the temptation and downfall of the upright woman.

It was a tempestuous day of early autumn. It not only rained, it poured! It not only blew, but it tore, howled, twisted, cavorted! The woman had to go to town. At the eleventh hour the family umbrella was kidnaped by a demon. (When the prince of evil has nothing else to do he sends out his imps to hide umbrellas, handkerchiefs, thimbles, scissors, and other domestic essentials.) The woman had no time to track the umbrella to its lair, so she pinned a newspaper over her bonnet and leaped for the train. Arrived in town she bought a 50 cent umbrella from a man who was peddling them on the street corner, and from that moment we date her downfall. The umbrella proved to be fashioned of gum arabic and cobweb. It leaked, it exuded, it faded away like a frost-flake in her hands, so that ere half an hour had passed she gave it to a newsboy, and laughed to see him kick it into an alley. Then she took off her plumed hat and pinned it underneath her cloak, wrapped a lace scarf about her head and proceeded on her way. Remarking the pleased expression on the faces of all she met, she wondered at it, with an Indian outbreak so imminent. Small boys danced by her in the rain to the sound of their own bright laughter; strong men seemed overcome as she drew near, and even the stern policemen at the street crossings turned aside to hide a 9x14 smile. The woman lunched at a popular restaurant in the midst of a mysterious carnival of glee, and finally took the train for home and, leaving the city limits, skirted the northern shores of the lake to the sound of muffled mirth. Reaching home and looking into the mirror she was confronted by a countenance that bore all the seeming "of a demon that is dreaming." The sea-green warp of cotton in the gum-arabic umbrella had melted and run in long lines over brow and nose and chin. For one moment the woman gazed at her frescoed charm, and as to what follows we will drop the curtain. Suffice it to say, she fell, and the shocked echoes of that little home put cotton in their ears and fainted into lonely space at being called upon to repeat the strong language that rent the air. Who shall blame the woman if she said "darn" with an emphasis that might have made a pirate wan with envy? Who shall cast the first stone at her until the day dawns that releases my sex from the thralldom of its bondage to those demons who walk abroad and plot her downfall in rainy weather?

Wear this bead upon your heart, girls; have nothing whatever to do with so-called "fascinating" or "magnetic" men. Put no faith in mystery when it comes to a question of the man you think you love. Rapt glances and tender sighs that lead to nothing in the way of an honest declaration are as despoiling to your womanhood as the breath of a furnace is to a flower. There is no mystery in genuine love, and there is no counterfeiting it, either. It is open-faced, ready-tongued and clear-eyed. It is a virtue for heroes, not a platitude in the mouth of fools. It is undefiled and set apart, like the snow on high hills. Allow no man to make you a party to anything clandestine. A man who is afraid to meet you at your own home, and appoints a tryst in the park, or a down-town restaurant, is as much of a menace to your happiness as a pestilence would be to your health. Remember, in all your experience with so-called love, that the fewer adventures a young woman has, the fewer flirtations and the fewer "affairs," the more glad she will be, by and by, when she is a good man's wife and a brave boy's or sweet girl's mother. A gown oft handled, you know, is seldom white, and each romance you weave with idle fellows who roll their eyes and talk love, but never show you the respect to offer you their hand in honest marriage—these fascinating "Rochesters" and wicked "St. Elmos," already married, or steeped to the lips in evil-doing—deprive you of your whiteness and your bloom.

Do you ever get discouraged and feel like saying: "Oh, it's no use! I want to amount to something! I have it in me to do great and grand things, but the circumstances of poverty are against me. I can be nothing but a drudge and the sooner I get over dreaming of anything higher, the better!" Of course you have just such times of thinking and talking, but did you ever comfort yourself with the thought that though all these things you can not be, you are, really, in the sight of God? A diamond is no less a diamond because it has been mislaid, and passed off through ignorance as common glass. A tulip seed is no less the sheath of a flower because through mistake somebody has labeled it as common timothy. A silk fabric is no less the product of the mulberry-feeding worm because somebody has wrapped it in a brown paper parcel and valued it as domestic jeans. What you are, you are, and there is no power on earth can gainsay it. Other folks may ignore it in you; half the world, nay all the world, may fail to see it, but if nobility, and strength, and sweetness are there you are worth just that much to God! Blessed thought, isn't it, you poor, overworked clerk, with your brain always in a muddle with the dry details of a business you hate! Blessed thought, isn't it, you dear, tired woman with more burdens to carry than a maple tree has leaves! No matter how impossible it may be for you to live out what is in you, that something true and grand and beautiful is deathless and shall have its chance of development by and by.

I shall never again meet the pretty maid with the larkspur eyes and the corn silk hair who traveled with us a part of the way, but wherever she goes, joy go with her! She was so modest and unspoiled and sweet, I declare the sight of such a girl in this day of dancers and high-steppers is like the sound of "Annie Laurie" between the carousals of a break-down jig, or the taste of a wild strawberry after pepper tea. God bless the old-fashioned girl with her helpful ways, her arch face and her blithe and hearty laugh. May her type never vanish from the face of the earth, and may the mold after which her soul was fashioned never get mislaid and lost in the heavenly work-shop.

I think I shall be a little sorry when the commanding officer sends out the word to break camp and leave this dear old earth forever. For I love this world. I never walk out in the morning when all its radiant colors are newly washed with dew, or at splendid noon, when, like an untired racer the sun has flashed around his mid-day course, or at evening, when a fringe of shadow, like the lash of a weary eye, droops over mountain and valley and sea, or in the majestic pomp of night when stars swarm together like bees and the moon clears its way through the golden fields as a sickle through the ripened wheat, that I do not hug myself for very joy that I am yet alive. The cruel grave has not got me! Those jaws of darkness have not swallowed me up, from the sweet light of mortal day! What matter if I am poor and unsheltered and costumeless? Thank God, I am yet alive! People who tire of this world before they are seventy and pretend that they are ready to leave it are either crazy or stuck full of bodily ailments as a cushion is of pins. The happy, the warm-blooded, the sunny-natured and the loving cling to life as petals cling to the calyx of a budding rose. By and by when the rose is over-ripe, or when the frosts come and the November winds are trumpeting through all the leafless spaces of the woods, will be the time to die. It is no time now, while there is a dark space left on earth that love can brighten, while there is a human lot to be alleviated by a smile, or a burden to be lifted with a sympathizing tear. It will be time to die when you are too old or too sick to be a comfort in the world, but if God has given you a warm heart and a ready hand, look about you and be glad He lets you live. Yesterday I was passing through the street and I saw a woman stoop down and pick up a faded lilac from the middle of a crossing and transfer it to a corner where it would not be trampled under foot. The world wants such people alive in it, not buried under its green sods. The heart that is not unmindful of a crushed flower will be a royal hand in the ministrations of life. May the day tarry long on its way that lays in the grave such helpful, tender hands that seek to do good.

The good book says, "Love thy neighbor as thyself," but it don't say, Tell thy neighbor all thy secrets. We can love one another without establishing an unsafe intimacy. In an age when so little remains set apart and sacred, keep the treasury of your inmost heart intact. It is a hard thing to believe that in every present friend is hidden a possible future enemy, but it is safer to shape the conduct of our life upon that belief than to live to see our inmost thoughts and the sanctities of one's heart of hearts hawked about like green peas in a street vender's basket by a spiteful and treacherous enemy. The safest course to pursue in a world so full of unfaith and desertions is to be friendly and sweet and helpful to all, but communicative and confiding to none.

Once when I was a child, with two long yellow braids down my back, and a very great capacity for happiness in my heart, I lived in a remote country with an aunt who didn't believe in any one having too good a time here on earth. She thought they would appreciate the new Jerusalem all the more, perhaps, for having a dismal experience here (there are lots like her, too, in the world to-day). Well, once afterward when I came home from school (and, ah! as I write how I can see the old road where I walked, winding its way under silver birches by the side of a trout-brook), somebody came out of the house and beckoned wildly, madly for me to hurry up. It was my little cousin, and she looked as though she had just skipped out of heaven! Her cheeks were all aglow and her eyes were shining like stars. "Oh, come!

Come quick!" she shouted. "There's something in the parlor." I made haste to enter, and there before me sat a doll, the biggest and most splendid it had ever entered my young heart to imagine. It was dressed in pink tarletan, and had a pair of jeweled earrings in its exceedingly life-like ears. At once I became embarrassed. Self-consciousness sprang into full being. I was painfully aware that my own dress and general appearance suffered by contrast with the doll. Nor have I ever since experienced a keener sensation of embarrassment than overcame me as I faced that gaudy image in wax. My aunt's sarcastic remark, "No wonder that child's mother can't lay up a cent for a rainy day when she throws away her dollars on a doll like that!" gave me the sad impression that my darling mother was a spendthrift, something after the pattern of the prodigal son. From the first moment the doll was a source of disappointment and sorrow to me. I never could play with it with any comfort because I was afraid of soiling its splendid clothes, losing its earrings, or feeling myself and my calico and homespun abashed by its superior attire. That doll did me no good, and just what it did for me its costly and extravagantly dressed sisterhood is doing for hundreds of little girls to-day. Too fine to be played with, rigged out in all its paraphernalia of empty headed flesh and blood women, with powder, puff and bustles, real jewelry and costly lingerie, the modern doll is a demoralizer, a torment.

Protracted broiling is, I think, on the whole, more wearing to the sensibilities than sudden conflagration. A lightning stroke is soon over, but who shall deliver us from the torments of dog-days? A bull of Bashan encountered in a ten-acre lot may be outrun, but who shall escape from a cloud of mosquitoes on a windless night? Give me any day a life to live with a tempestuous, gusty sort of person, and I can endure it, but deliver me from existence with one who bottles up his thunder and looks like a storm that never breaks. A hearty shower, beating down the flowers to call them up again in fresher beauty, brightening the hills and swelling the brooks, treading with musical footfall the dusty streets, and lashing the violet-tinted lake into a foam-flecked sea, veining the hot air with sudden fire, and calling out a thousand echoes to answer the thunder's call, is it not far better than lowering skies that look rain and won't yield it, dragging, sultry days of neither sunshine nor storm?

LINES TO MY LOVE.

When the salt has left the ocean,
  And the moon forgets the sea,
When with gay and festive motion
  Ox shall waltz with bee,

When we wash our face in cinders,
  And bake our meat on ice,
When tender mercy hinders
  The cat from eating the mice,

When gray heads grace young shoulders
  And icicles form in June,
When Quakers all turn soldiers,
  And bull frogs sing in tune,

Then, and not till then, my treasure,
  My darling, tender and true,
My heart shall claim the leisure
  To think no more of you.

The other morning, lured by the splendor of a golden day, I started to walk to town, a distance of twenty-four miles. But after the tenth mile the truth was so forcibly and increasingly borne in upon me that "all flesh is grass," and that the strength of a man (or woman either) "lieth not in his heels," that I postponed the finish until another day. But who shall take from me the glory of the start? Shall anybody forget that a sunrise was fair and full of promise because the noon was clouded and the evening declined into rain? Although my twenty-five-mile walk ended at the tenth in a rocking-chair, yet those ten miles were beautiful and full of glory.

"It will certainly kill you!" wailed the martyr as I bade her good-bye. "Oh, will it kill her?" echoed the poor little Captain, and lifted up her voice in lamentation as I vanished from her sight and struck for the bluff road. The morning was so beautiful that I could imagine the world nothing but a big bunch of tulips standing within a crystal vase in the sun. The maples glistened like gold, and were flecked with ruby drops that burned and glowed like spilled wine. The oaks were russet brown and dusky purple, cleft here and there with vivid green, like glimpses of a windy sea through shadowed hills. The leaves that had fallen to the earth were musical underneath the foot, and gave forth a faint fragrance that made the air as sweet as any bakeshop. The odor of fallen leaves and wood shrubs sinking into decay is not like any other fragrance so much as the scent of well-baked bread, browned and finished in summer's ruddy heat.

The lake—but what can I say to fitly describe that translucent sapphire, over which a mist hung like a gossamer web above a blue-bell, or the haze of slumber upon a drowsy eye? As I stood upon the bluff, before the road struck landward through the woods, I could but extend my arm to the glorious expanse of waters and bless the Lord with all my soul for so lovely a place to tarry in between times. If this world is only a stopping-place, a country through which we march to heaven, as Sherman marched overland to the sea, then thank God for so glorious a prelude to eternity; and what shall the after harmonies be when the broken sounds of idly-touched flutes and harps are so divine?

After leaving Ravinia I proceeded to get

lost in the woods. A very small boy and a very large dog were standing by a fence. "Does that dog bite?" I asked. "Yes'm," promptly replied the sweet and candid child. So I climbed a fence and struck for the timber. I soon found that all knowledge of the points of the compass had failed me. "If I am going east," I mused, "I shall soon strike the lake; if west, the track; south will eventually bring me to the Chicago River; but a northerly direction will restore me to the sleuth-hound. I will say my prayers and endeavor to keep to the south." The way grew denser. My hat gave me some trouble, as it insisted upon hanging itself to every tree in the wilderness. The twigs twitched the hair-pins from my hair and poked themselves into my eyes. A few corpulent bugs toyed with my ankles and a large caterpillar passed the blockade of my collar-button and basked in the warmth of my neck. I nearly stepped on a snake and was confronted by a toad that froze me with a glance of its basilisk eye. So I changed my course and suddenly entered a little woodland graveyard—a handful of neglected mounds of earth and silence. No tombstones marked the graves. A rudely-constructed cross of wood, gray with lichens, alone told of consecrated ground. There, away off from the road in the silence of the woods, a few tired hearts were taking their rest. Silently I stood a moment, then stole away and left the place to its hush of lonely peace. What right had I, with my frets and feathers, my twig-punctured eye-balls and my toad-perturbed nerves, to bring an unquiet presence within this abode of silence and of rest? I sat down on a fence-rail a moment while, like Miss Riderhood, I deftly twisted up my back hair and mused briefly. When the time comes, oh, intensely alive and happy Amber, for your feet to halt in the march, ask to be buried in the woods, where your grave will be forgotten and the constant years with falling leaves and driving snows may have a good chance to obliterate the earthly record of your misspent years.

"Sooner or later the shadows shall creep
Over my rest in the woods so deep;
Sooner or later—"

But enough of this, my dear. I did not intend to incorporate a whole cemetery, an obituary discourse, and "lines to the departed" in my "Glints." After leaving the little graveyard I allowed my instincts to carry me in a new direction, and soon a rustling among the dead leaves, and the sound of hushed breathing, convinced me that I was approaching a living presence. I felt for my revolver. It was there, but unloaded. (I would sooner walk arm in arm with death than carry loaded firearms.) I advanced bravely and became speedily aware of a score or so of large and startled eyes, all fixed upon me. A half-score of woolly heads were lifted, and a flock of sheep stood ready to take instant flight if I showed sign of battle. "My dear young friends," said I, "it is a relief to meet you, and I give you good morrow. I fully expected to encounter a band of cutthroat tramps who should toss pennies for my heart's blood. The blessings of a rescued woman rest upon your crinkly coats, my beauties." A half-hour's walk through the woods brought me to a clearing where a flock of bluebirds were holding council together among the falling leaves. They seemed inclined to start southward, but tarried for one last frolic. How beautiful they were as they flitted in and out among the golden underbrush no eye but mine shall ever know. Bluebirds have always been associated with thoughts of spring and apple-blossoms heretofore. I could hardly believe my senses to find them here amid the late and falling leaves. For a while I loitered in their midst and wished for a fairy to change me into one of their winged company, that I might forget care and find no need of revolvers; but time, as sternly announced by my exquisite Waterbury, admitted of no delay, so I hied me onward. At this point in my walk I approached a broken gate and a stretch of shockingly muddy road. The vanity of confidence in any strength that emanates alone from the "heels of a man" was by this time beginning to make itself felt. I longed to sit down in the miry way and go to sleep. A child could have played with me despite my revolver, and a day-old lamb have gained the victory in a personal encounter. At this moment, while I lingered, picking my way daintily from tuft to tuft of the swamp, I was confronted by a tall, gaunt woman. Of course you don't believe this; it reads too much like a dime novel. You think I am painting my picture in lurid tints for public exhibition, but in spite of your incredulity I repeat that I was confronted by a tall, gaunt woman, who appeared as suddenly as though invoked by an evil spell from the mud. The woman was shabbily dressed and wore an old-fashioned scoop bonnet. She had a bundle on her arm, and was dragging by the hair of the head, as it were, an indescribable umbrella. My voice sank out of sight, like a stone in the sea, and my feet grew too heavy to lift. I stared in silence. "Is your name Maria Hopkins?" asked the woman.

"Indeed it is," I replied, prepared to get down on my knees and swear to the truth of what I said, if need be. "I thought so," said my companion; "let us pray." But I didn't stop for prayers. Convinced that my time had come, and that I was in the presence of a lunatic, I fell over the fence and ran. When I was out of breath I looked over my shoulder, but the woman was nowhere in sight. To pursue my walk seemed unnecessary, especially as I was nearing the house of a friend, so summoning what strength was left me I toddled onward, completing my tenth mile in five hours from the starting. After my sympathizing friend had emptied her camphor bottle upon me I asked her if she knew a party of the name of Hopkins anywhere in town, and if there was any resemblance between such a person and myself. I saw she thought I was delirious, and no explanation has ever dispelled that belief. Some day I shall complete the walk and write up the finish.

Said some one to me the other day: "Amber, you have lots of good friends among the girls." "Good," said I; "then I am all right." Anybody who gains the friendly approval of the right sort of girls has a passport right through to glory! I mean it. There is nothing on earth I love better than a good, sweet girl. I would rather watch a crowd of them any day than all the pictures Fra Angelica ever painted of saints in paradise. But there are girls and girls. There is as much difference between them as there is between griddle cakes made with yeast and griddle cakes in which the careless cook forgot to put the leaven. Shall I tell you the kind of girl I especially adore? Well, first of all, let us take the working girl. She is not a "lady" in the acceptance of the term by this latter day's hybrid democracy. She is just a blithe, cheery, sweet-tempered young woman. She may have a father rich enough to support her at home, but for all that she is a working girl. She is never idle. She is studying or sewing or helping about the home part of the day. She is romping or playing or swinging out of doors the other part. She is never frowsy nor untidy nor lazy. She is never rude nor slangy nor bold. And yet she is always full of fun and ready for frolic. She does not depend upon a servant to do what she can do for herself. She is considerate to all who serve her. She is reverent to the old and thoughtful of the feeble. She never criticises when criticism can wound, and she is ready with a helpful, loving word for every one. Sometimes she has no father, or her parents are too poor to support her. Then she goes out and earns her living by whatever her hands find to do. She clerks in a store, or she counts out change at a cashier's desk, or she teaches school, or she clicks a typewriter, or rather a telegrapher's key, but always and everywhere she is modest and willing and sweet, provided she doesn't get that meddlesome little "bee" of "lady"-hood in her bonnet. If she tries to be a lady at the expense of all that is honest and frank in her nature, she is like a black baby crying for a black kitten in the dark—you can't tell what she is exactly, but you know she is mighty disagreeable. She has too much dignity to be imposed upon, or put to open affront, but she has humility also, and purity that differs from prudishness as a dove in the air differs from a stuffed bird in a showcase. She is quick to apologize when she knows she is in the wrong, yet no young queen ever carried a higher head than she can upon justifiable occasions. She is not always imagining herself looked down upon because she is poor. She knows full well that out of her own heart and mouth proceed the only witnesses that can absolve or condemn her. If she eats peanuts in public places, and talks loud, and flirts with strange boys, and chews gum or displays a toothpick she is common, even though she wore a four-foot placard emblazoned with the misnomer, "lady." If she is quick to be courteous, unselfish, gentle and retiring in speech and manner in public places, she is true gold, even though her dress be faded and her bonnet be old. You cannot mistake any girl any more than you can mistake the sunshine that follows the rain or the lark that springs from the hawthorn hedge. All things that are blooming and sweet attend her! The earth is better for her passing through it and heaven will be fairer for her habitation therein. God bless her!

Some day I am going gunning. In a reform dress suit, with the right to vote in my pocket, and a shotgun delicately poised upon my enfranchised shoulder, I shall start forth on my "safety" and proceed to lay low for a few victims. The first to perforate with my murderous bullet shall be the fiend in human guise who toys with my "copy" from time to time and makes me spell whether without an "h," or so distorts the sense of what I write that my best friends wouldn't know me from Martin Tupper. I shall show no mercy to him. I shall continue to shoot until he is perforated like a yard of mosquito netting, and I shall leave a little note pinned to the lapel of his coat saying that I have more bullets left for his "successor in trust." If there is one thing that has survived the buffetings of a harsh and somewhat disconcerting bout with fate it is the knowledge that I know how to spell. But even of this the fiend in question would deprive me. He has brought his fate upon himself and will excuse me if I remark that I thirst for his gore.

Dominated by that superfluous energy which has, so far, rendered my earthly career cyclonic, I called together a confiding band during the height of the recent snow carnival for the purpose of a sleigh ride. The opening up of that sleigh ride was propitious. The caravan moved due north, bound for a destination that shall be nameless. We tried to look upon the attention we attracted as a public ovation, but it was far more suggestive of the way they used to accompany outlaws beyond the limits of a mining town, or of the children of Israel chased by Pharaoh's mocking hosts. It was cold. Our noses, in the light of a wan old moon, looked like doorknobs. Our ears cracked to the lightest touch, like harp strings in the wind. Patient, long-suffering "doctor!" Shall I ever forget how, turning to him when the carnival of sport was at its height, I murmured: "Are you enjoying yourself, dear?" And he replied, with ghastly sarcasm: "Tumultuously, my love!" So might an arctic frigate, ice-bound, have hailed a polar bear. Suddenly, when all seemed progressing serenely, we came to a standstill, something like what might be expected from a runaway horse checked by the newly patented electric button. What was the matter? Bare ground. Now, under ordinary circumstances, the term "bare ground" is not synonymous of disaster. But if ever in the dispensation of providence it falls to your lot to be one of a band of sleigh-riding imbeciles then shall those two words be to you what snags in the channel are to seaward-hastening keels. The driver shouted and became distinctly profane. "Would you please get out and walk over this bad place?" said he. With such speed as our petrified members would allow we all got out, and the women sat on a wayside fence, while the men "heaved to" and dragged the chariot over about a mile and a quarter of bare ground.

"Shall we make for the nearest line of

street cars?" asked one of the party, whose well-known position as Sunday-school superintendent kept him in a state of abnormal calm. "What will become of the sleigh and the poor, tired horses?" asked that one of the party directly responsible for this mad jubilee.

"Oh, you women can lead the horses while we men carry the old band wagon on our shoulders back to shelter." "It is no time for jokes," cried one, "I am going home," and we all followed suit, to vow later, in the shelter of our happy homes, that our future attempts at sleigh riding should be confined to wheels and the time of roses.

I think I would rather lose this serviceable old right hand of mine than have it write a word that could be construed into defense or encouragement of loud and blatant women. The over-dressed and slangy sisterhood who parade in public places and storm the land these latter days will meet with nothing from Amber and her pen but wholesale denunciation while the lamp of an insignificant life holds out to burn. I hate them as a

Quaker hates gunpowder, and I am more than half inclined to believe that the total extermination of the stock would be one of the supremest blessings that could be vouchsafed to man. The tendencies toward boldness and effrontery which characterize the present day, the unabashed speech and action and the manifest lack of old-fashioned courtesy and the reserve that springs from gentle breeding are evils that grow rather than diminish. A gentlewoman, a pure, correct and lovely gentlewoman, occupies a loftier place than any throne, and wields an influence more potent than the swing of a jeweled scepter. Yet it is never by vulgar assumption that she enters into her kingdom. The parrot is not a bird we prize, although its plumage is resplendent with green and purple and gold. In the proud breast of the homely and unpretentious thrush is hidden the heavenly song. Wherever gentle forbearance is found, wherever patience and tenderness and love idealize and sweeten life, there you will find woman as heaven meant she should be—the crowned queen of hearth and home. And in saying all this I do not wish to be understood as advancing the idea that a woman has no wider scope than home, or that she must be all sugar, without any spice. Next to the loud and bold-mannered woman as a specimen to be detested I would put the meek Griselda, with less spirit than a boneless herring and less sparkle than tepid tea. There is no charm left to femininity when you add idiocy to a pretty woman's make-up. A fool may be very docile, but a fool is not good company. Of the two, perhaps, if a man were forced to choose a comrade to share a life that was to be cast on a South Sea island, he would do better to take the "loud" type. Either would drive him to the "cups," if such relief were to be found upon an island of the sea. But who would not rather go to wreck in a storm than founder in becalmed waters? Or, to bring it nearer home, who would not rather be drowned away out in the middle of Lake Michigan in a howling gale than in a gentle 7x9 cistern? If circumstances call a woman out into the thickest of the old bread-and-butter fight that has been waging ever since Eve ran afoul of the apple, it is to her credit if she rolls up her sleeves and goes into the thickest of the scrimmage and holds her own with the pluckiest of them all. It is no disgrace to her to be quick to seize an opportunity and shrewd to find a point of vantage. Let her rank with the men, and make ever so fine a name for herself in whatever business vocation she chooses to make her own, it will not detract one whit from her womanliness, provided she keep herself unsullied of soul and tender of heart. The moment she lends herself to practices that lead men to forget to touch their hats when she passes by she becomes unsexed, and a sexless woman is worse than a pestilence, a cyclone and a strike condensed into one vast calamity. No sensible man will think any less of a woman if she has spirit enough to get downright mad at injustice, insult or iniquity. I don't know, though, why we women should always get together and compare notes as to what course of conduct will best please the men. They don't lie awake nights to conform their behavior to ways and manners that shall please us; but, even putting our argument on the basis of what shall win approval from men, I repeat that I don't believe that there are many of them who would object to a woman knowing how to use a pistol or to her carrying one in case of an unprotected walk, or a night spent in an unguarded home. There would be fewer tales to tell of assaults and woful disappearances of young women if all our girls were versed in the ethics of the revolver. Ah, my dear, you can never get a more adorable portrait of a woman to hang upon the walls of glorified fancy than the pen-portrait drawn by the master hand of Robert Browning when he wrote of beautiful Evelyn Hope: "God made her of spirit, fire and dew." There is the swiftest and most splendid stroke of the artist's brush ever given to literature. And yet half the world would substitute "putty" for "spirit," "feathers" for "fire" and "dough" for "dew."

The only way to rid the world of bubble-marriages—marriages that turn out emptiness with one drop of water as the residuum, and that drop a tear—is to educate our girls and boys to something higher than playing with pipes and soapy water. Give them something more earnest to do, and see that they do it. Compel men and women to choose their life companions with at least a tithe of the solemnity they bring to the se-

Rosemary and Rue. 241

lection of a carriage horse or a ribbon. Legislate laws against early marriages. "I can't tolerate children," said a little idiot to me the other day, "but I adore dogs!" And yet that girl had an engagement ring on her finger. There should be a special seclusion for such girls until they develop some instinct of womanliness, and they should no more be allowed to marry than a Choctaw chief should be allowed to take charge of a kindergarten. You nor I can hope to turn a bubble into substance after it is once blown.

❧

Last week I moved. At least I tried to, but I haven't fully accomplished the feat yet. If it costs one woman a desk and an umbrella, the pangs of a seven-horse torment to move one block, what must it cost a family of fourteen to move seven wagonloads a mile? There is a problem that will keep you awake nights. When they said to me: "Oh, it will be nothing for you to move!" When they pointed with derision at my few belongings I said to myself: "All right; perhaps it will be easier than my fears." So I packed up my penknife, my mucilage pot, my paper cutter, my eleven dozen pencils and my assortment of stub pens, my violet ink, my clock, pictures, calendars, Japanese fans, scraps of poetry, magazines, books, lemons, buttercups, blotting pads, and sundry trifles it were waste of time to enumerate, and sallied forth to find a son of wrath to transport them to new quarters. "How much will you charge to move two articles of furniture one block?" I asked a guileless Scandinavian teamster. "Three dollars," replied he with touching promptitude. I passed him by, and after two days' search found a down-trodden African who said he would undertake the job for $1.50. I wish you could have seen the look in the darky's face when he tried to lift the desk. "Gor-a-mighty, Missus, what's in that ar desk?" cried he. I had to unpack every blessed article but the penknife and a postage stamp before he would move the thing, and all the long day I trotted back and forth with market baskets full of the original contents of that desk. When at last I had them moved I couldn't find anything. I wanted my pencils, but haven't seen 'em yet. The paperweight had smashed the ink bottle, and the mucilage had formed a glassy pool in which my buttercups were anchored like islands. The frizzes and hairpins and other little what-nots that I kept in the right hand drawer had dabbled themselves in the ink and mucilage and fused themselves into one indistinguishable horror. I haven't been able to find one thing that I wanted since I moved but a toothpick, and that don't look exactly natural. The overshoes, and gossamer, and jersey waists, soap and chamois skins that I secreted in the left hand drawer haven't been seen since they left in the market basket under convoy of the Ethiopian. He has probably opened a costumer's shop on Halsted street with them. When I move again I shall carry my pencils behind my ear and my penknife between my teeth. I'll never be found a second time stringing my beads with a toothpick and relying for time upon a clock with the hour hand missing. When next I move may it be straight through to glory, where the lease is long and the landlord never sublets.

Let anybody in this world really undertake to thoroughly do his duty; to do it in the face of opposition, prejudice and the meddling interference of fools, and he becomes a target set upon a hill for the convenient aim of popular scorn. It is harder for a man to be true to a principle than it is to face a gun. If an employe in the daily discharge of duty aims to be prompt, faithful and fearless he is boycotted by his associates in almost as conspicuous a way as was poor little David Copperfield with the pasteboard motto on his back. We all of us have known in early life the "pet scholar" of the school, the dear little virtuous prig who never did anything out of the way, who never played a prank or accomplished anything but a pattern pose. Small wonder that we hated him! Good behavior, which has for its aim merely the disconcerting of others and the aggrandizement of one's self, is snobbery and should be loathed as such. But there is a courage of over-conviction which leads a man to hold himself honest among thieves, pure among libertines and faithful among time-servers and strikers. It was such a spirit as this that made dear little "Tom," at "Rugby," loyal to his mother's teachings, and led him to kneel amid a crowd of jeering boys to say the prayers she taught him. It is such a spirit as this that holds a man or woman true to the sense of justice in an unjust world, and keeps them undaunted in the midst of enemies, who hate them for doing their duty and caring as much for the work as they do for the wages that work commands. The man who can hold himself beyond the reach of bribery, uncorrupted in corruptible times, and sure to keep his colors flying, with never a chance to trail them in the dust for politic purposes, is a greater hero than many a blue-coat who marches to battle. Give us a few more such heroes, oh, good and merciful dispenser of destinies, and sweep off the track a hundred thousand or so of the eye-servants, time-servers and money-graspers who keep the profitable places of the world's giving away from honest men and faithful women.

A BOBOLINK'S SONG.

The earth was awake, and like a gay rover,
  His knapsack of sunshine loose strapped on his back,
Through mists, and through dews, and through fine purple clover
  Was faring his way down the summer's green track.

Rosemary and Rue.

I sat all alone 'neath the shade of a willow,
   And saw the old earth blithely jogging along,
While over the fields, like the foam on a billow,
   The morning was breaking in blossom and song.

O, list! and, O, hear! like the wing of a swallow,
   Updarting from fields that are golden with corn;
With the ring and the swing of a huntsman's "view hallo,"
   Some fairy is winding his sweet elfin horn.

Now up like a flame, and now down like a shower;
   Now here and now there in its sparkle and gloom;
It rings and it swings like a bell in a tower,
   Wide casting its notes as a wind-flower its bloom.

'Tis a bobolink singing among the sweet clover;
   A bobolink whimsical, happy and free,
And its voice like new wine makes earth, the old rover,
   Half tipsy with jollity, clean daft with his glee.

It fell to my lot the other day to witness a scene that I shall not soon forget. Death has myriad ways of coming to the sons and daughters of men, and it chanced that death had drawn near to a certain dear woman in a way that well might blanch the cheek of the bravest hero. As surely condemned to die as is the murderer when he hears the judge's sentence, with absolute hopelessness of any cure, and with the certainty of no more than a brief span of weeks wherein to live, this brave woman faced her doom with all the condemned man's certainty, and yet without his shame. Grown old in a life of peculiar usefulness, with not a single abated enthusiasm and with a heart as keenly attuned to nature's as is the flute to the master's touch, this dear old heroine calmly renounced the world she had so loved and turned her face direct to "headquarters," with no friend to interfere between herself and God. For one bitter hour, perhaps, she wept and watched alone in her Gethsemane, then turned about to await the chariot wheels of her deliverance with a heart as glad and a faith as warm and bright as a little child's who waits in the shadow the coming of a loving father to lead her home. Taken to the hospital to die, knowing that those doors swung for her last entrance within any earthly home, fully realizing that from beneath that roof her soul should ascend to its home beyond the stars, bidding good-bye forever to the sunset skies and the rural walks that she had so loved, to all the bright company of wild flowers she had known by name, to the pomp of seasons and the communion of happy homes, she took up her abode in the ward of the incurables. Every day she sits in the sunshine and reads her books or indites letters to her friends. Every day she struggles with devastating pain, and every day she grows a little thinner and a little weaker in the body, while her soul springs heavenward like a white flower from the dust, which no earthly blight can reach. As I sat by her side the other morning and held her wasted hand in mine it seemed the most natural thing in the world to send a message by this sweet soul to the unseen land, and we almost forgot the pain of parting in the bright anticipation of the many who would throng to meet the gray-headed voyager when at last her sail should beat across the blue waters into the heavenly harbor. And as we talked there came a message that a very old friend had called to see the sufferer; one who had been the closest comrade of her brilliant youth and the companion of her maturer years. Slowly the guest entered the shrine wherein a soul awaited the sacrament of death, silently she stretched out her arms and gathered that wasted frame within their close embrace. As a mother comforts the baby at her breast, so they comforted one another with tender words. The years of their life fell away from them as petals from a rose which the wind lightly rocks, and they were girls again. "Oh, my dear child, how sweet, how brave, how grand you are!" said the guest. "My precious girl, my poor, dear one, how can I bear to see you here!" she cried again and yet again, while her tears fell like rain, and the turmoil of her sobs rent her very inmost heart. I shall live long before I see so touching a sight again. In the presence of a love so perfect and so true I felt to be almost an interloper and an alien, so I quietly stole away and left these two old women, bowed with the weight of many years, sustaining and sustained by the trust that the portals of the tomb, within whose shadows they stood, were but the gates that usher the soul into the full affluence of life and love.

It is almost impossible to get the average young person past the florist's window nowadays. She has a way of clasping her hands and pursing her lips over the roses that would make the average young man shed his last dollar, as the almond tree shakes its blossoms. I am always sorry for a poor young man in love with a pretty girl. He longs to buy the world for her and she longs quite as ardently to receive it as a gift, and so he is hurrying along his bankrupt career until matrimony or estrangement checks him. Have you not a pitying remembrance in your own heart of a certain youth of the long ago who deluged your house with roses, confectionery and novels until his salary was wildly wasted in the unequal contests? Girls, be a little less receptive, as it were; be just a bit more thoughtful and delicate in your orders at the restaurant and your selection from the florist's window, and I think your matrimonial chances will be the better for it. How often have I seen a young woman order a costly dinner when some young man whom she well knew to be the recipient of a small salary was to foot the bill, yet when ordering for herself I am told she never goes higher than beans and bread and butter. Now, girls, don't think Amber is an everlasting old grandmother! Not a bit of it, but she has tossed about the world so much and heard so many "little birds" telling their secrets that she has taken unto herself quite a pack of knowledge of the ways and manners of mankind. I positively adore a young girl, and always have, and, what is more, expect I always shall. But admiring and loving them as I do, from the tip of their bangs to the click of their boot heels, I cannot bear to see them do unlovely things. I want to see them helpful, lovable, sweet. I want to see them slow to wound another's feelings, and quick as sunshine after rain with tender smiles and womanly ways. I want to see them brave, yet gentle; gay, yet kind; fun-loving, yet never loud and rude. I want to hear the young men in speaking of them speak of something besides their extravagance and their greed. I want the very air to be the sweeter for their passing, as when one carries roses through a room their fragrance lingers. And what shall make you sweet, dear girls? Not fashionable gowns and dainty clothing; not beauty nor grace nor wealth so much as womanliness and unselfish thought for others.

The woman who can wear an arctic overshoe over a No. 5 shoe and make no moan ought to have been born a Joan of Arc or a Charlotte Corday. She is made of the "dust" that heroines have a corner on. At one time in my life I owned a dog—a guileless pup—whose darling aim on earth was to drag my colossal arctics before admiring gentlemen callers and lay them by the fireside, where they overshadowed the big baseburner with their bulk. I was rid of the dog long before I was rid of the feeling that it was a disgrace for a woman to wear the feet God gave her. The most colossal overshoe is neither so big nor so objectionable as an early grave, and that is just what lies before some of you girls if you don't quit wearing French heels and going about in damp and chilly weather without protection for your feet. Burn up the high-heeled slippers, then, with their atrocious shape; cultivate health and common-sense rather than the empty flattery of a world that cares nothing for you. So shall you be as beautiful as houris, as healthy as Hebes, as long lived as

Sarahs and as light-footed as the shadow that dances to a wind-blown Columbine.

A graveyard never saddens me. It seems nothing more than one of the flies behind the scenes when the actors have gone on in front. What matters the room where we doff our toggery when we are once out of it? So, not long since, when in rambling about one of the Apostle Islands, away up in Lake Superior country, I ran across a sunshiny little graveyard, and I was glad to loiter about for an hour and read the inscriptions on the age-worn stones. It was a blue day—blue in the sky above and blue in the haze on the hills, blue in the sparkling waters of the lake and bluer yet in the far distance that marked a score of miles from shore. Before the gateway of the graveyard a clump of golden rod stood, like an angel barring the way with a sword of light. A tangle of luxuriant vines had curtained most of the graves from sight. A few, more carefully tended than the rest, stood bravely out from behind fences of ornamental woodwork, but most of them were sheltered and peaceful within their neglected bowers of green. When my time comes to lie down in my narrow home, I pray you, kind gentlefolks, grant me the seclusion of an unremembered grave rather than the accentuated desolation of a painted fence and a padlocked gate. There is rest in neglect, and nature, if left alone, will never allow a grave to grow unsightly. She folds it away in added coverings of mossy green from year to year as a mother when the nights are long will tuck her sleeping children under soft, warm blankets. She appoints her choristers from the leafy belfry of the woods to keep the chimes ringing when the days are long and slow and sweet, and lights her tapers nightly in the wavering shimmer of the stars. In a secluded corner we found a handbreadth space where a baby was laid to rest many a year ago. No chronicle of the little life remains, and yet a stranger stands beside its grave and drops a tear. I don't know why, I'm sure, for why should we cry when a baby dies? So roses are picked before the frost finds them! Another stone was erected to a young bride who died at twenty. Looking about at the stoop-shouldered, care-lined and prematurely old women who toiled in those island homes, we could not feel very sorry for the young bride who died, perhaps, while life still held an illusion. With lingering step at last we left the graveyard, repassed the golden sentry at the gate and sought the little boat that awaited us on the beautiful bay. Long after other details of that pleasant outing are forgotten the memory of that blue day among the quiet graves on the island of the great lake shall linger like a song within our hearts.

"If I had two loaves of bread," said Mahomet, "I would sell one of them and buy white hyacinths, for they would feed my soul." I came across that delightful saying the other day, and I thought to myself: There is another one to be hunted up when I get over yonder! I shall have to make the acquaintance of a man, prophet or not, who gave utterance to such a sentiment as that. How many of us, poor earthworms that we are, would rather spend our dollar for white hyacinths than for a big supper? How many of us ever stop to think that there is something under the sleek rotundity of our girth that demands food quite as eagerly as our stomach does, and fails and faints and dies quite as surely without it? Take less of the food that goes to fatten the perishable part of you, and give more sustenance to that inner guest who, like a captive, sits and starves with long and cruel neglect. Buy fewer glasses of beer and more "white hyacinths." Smoke less tobacco and invest in a few sunsets and dawns. Let cheap shows alone and go hear music of the right sort. So shall your soul lift up its drooping head and grow less and less to resemble one of Pharaoh's lean kine. I adore a man or a woman who has enough sentiment to appreciate what dead and gone Mahomet said, and hereafter will make it a point to buy less bread and more hyacinths.

I wonder if, when we get to the other world, we shall not occasionally stroll into some sort of a celestial museum, where the relics of our foregone existence, its wasted days and misspent years, may stare back at us from glass cases where the angels have ticketed them and put them all neatly on exhibition! There will be necklaces of ill-spent moments, like the faded brilliants exhumed from old Pompeii, with lots of broken hopes and thwarted destinies. There will be odd little freaks and unreasoning caprices, like the "What is it?" and foolish deeds of daring to turn our pulses faint with the old-time terror. There will be those tendencies which kept us heavy-footed like the fat woman, and others that made us blind, although the world was full of light. There will be the disloyal deeds that made us a constant source of care and wonderment to the angels who watched us, and the cowardice that kept us in leading strings to conformity. There will be shelves full of the little white lies we have told, all labeled and dated, like pebbles from the Mediterranean or bits of shell from the sea. There will be fragments of blighted lives ruined by wagging tongues and shafts of tea table gossip. There will be the old-time masks wherein we masqueraded, and the flimsy veils of deceit behind which we hid our individuality. There will be the memories of little children we might have kept had we been wiser, and snatches of lullaby songs. There will be jars full of love glances and pots of preserved and honeyed kisses. There will be whole bales of mistakes, a Gobelin tapestry to drape the world, and stacks of dead and withered "might-have-beens." There will be peacock feathers of pride tied together with faded ribbons of regret, and whole cabinets full of closet skeletons and family contentions. There will be pedestals whereon shall stand the "white days" we can never forget, and panorama chambers wherein shall be unrolled the pictured scroll of our journey heavenward. In cunningly devised music boxes we shall hear again the melody of our youthful laughter and the patter of life's uncounted tears. I think the shelves of that celestial museum would yield some odd surprises to the most of us, like the finding of a bauble we counted worthless and threw away glittering in the diadem of a crown, or the prize we bartered honor for turned to worthless glitter and tinsel paste!

There is no use sitting here by this window any longer and trying to believe that life is worth living. If I looked for five minutes more at this November landscape I should shave my head and hie me to a Carmelite convent. Dame Nature has forgotten her housewifely duties and gone off to gossip with the good ladies who have charge of the other planets. Where but yesterday the late asters bloomed in long rows of splendor, and the chrysanthemums fringed the sunny borders with feathers of white and gold, the unsightly stalks grovel in the clayey mold, and the frost-nipped vines drop their dismantled tendrils in the chilly wind. Fragments of old china lurk in the discovered spaces underneath the denuded lilac bushes, and out by the oleander tub a cruel cat is worrying a large and discouraged rat. That oleander tub reminds me an ordeal that is ushered in with every change of season. Twice a year we are compelled to carry that large vegetable in and out of its winter lair. About the last week of September we begin to wrap it in bed-quilts every night, and from that time on until late autumn no delicate babe was ever more tenderly guarded. Then, as there is no man in the country who for love or lucre will condescend to the job, we begin to worry the Doctor. We tell him the oleander will be blighted by the frost, and he pays no heed. Then we ask him if he would just as lief bring in the oleander after supper. He sneaks off and is gone until the 11 p. m. train. Next we take to tears, and declare that we love that oleander as one of the family, and it breaks our heart to see it perish for want of care. We grow pale and wan and gray-headed as the days go by, and finally with flashing eyes and muttered oaths the Doctor yanks the tub and its colossal growth into the cellar, and we rest on our arms until the advent of another spring.

Well, the summer has gathered up her corn-silk draperies, put on her rose-trimmed hat, and tripped over the border land at last. From the bend in the road that shall hide her from our view forever she lingers a moment to throw back a sunny glance at September, as he comes whistling down the lane, with plume of golden-rod in his hat. A glad good-bye to you, long-to-be-remembered summer of 1890! We are so glad to see you go that we are willing to forego your blossoms and your bird songs to be well rid of you. For three long months we have endured heat without precedent, drought and discomfort, flies and mosquitos, threatened thunder gusts and devastating cyclones, and we are so tired that we feel like shaking a stick at you now, to see you lingering to coquet with September. Hasten on, oh bright autumn weather, with your comfortable nights for sleep, and your royal days of sunshine and frost. We are longing for the time to come when the lamps shall be lighted early in the parlor, and the fire-glow shall once more shed its glory upon grandma's lovely hair and upon the gold of the children's restless heads; when the cat shall have leave to lie on the best cushion, and the voice of the tea-kettle, droning its supper monologue, shall alternate with the efforts of the older sister at the piano. By the way, do you know there is lots of solace to be found in an old music book of twenty years ago? Don't tell me that the music of to-day is as sweet all through as the melodies of long ago. Who sings such soul-ravishing duets to-day as "She Bloomed with the Roses," "Twilight

Dews," or "Gently Sighs the Breeze"? I declare to you, my dear, that although I shall be considerably older some day than I am now, and although I have not fallen so far into the "sere and yellow" as to count myself among the old-fashioned and the queer, yet any one of those songs just mentioned will start the tears from my eyes as showers start from summer clouds.

Two little motherless children! Do you know the thought of a baby without a mother to cuddle it always brings the tears to my eyes? Traveling to distant New England with a father who, although kind, seemed some way unfitted to his duties, as a straight-legged chair might if used for a lullaby rocker, were two bits of folks, a boy and a girl, one four, the other two years old. The careful father brushed their hair very nicely and washed their mites of faces with great regularity. When he told them to sit still they sat still, and nobody was annoyed by their antics, but, oh, how it made my heart ache to watch the motherless chicks! If mamma had been there they would have climbed all over her, and bothered her a good deal, perhaps, with their clinging arms and kisses (it's a way babies have with their mammas!), but in the presence of their dark-eyed and quiet papa they behaved like little weasels in the presence of a fox. "Papa says we mustn't talk about mamma any more," lisped the boy. "'Cause she's gone to heaven." In the name of love, whose apostle I humbly claim to be, I longed to gather those little ones in my arms and have a dear, sweet talk about the mamma who had left them for a little while, and I wanted to say to the proper and punctilious papa: "Good sir, if you attempt to bring up these motherless mites without the demonstration of love you will meet with the same success your gardener would should he set out roses in a pine forest. Children need love as flowers need the southerly exposure and sunshine. When that boy of yours bumped his head, sir, it was your place to comfort him in something the way his dead mother might have done, rather than to have bade him 'sit up and be a man.'"

SLEEP'S SERENADE.

In cadence far,
From star to star,
Sleep's mellow horns are faintly calling;
Through dreamland halls
Sweet madrigals,
In liquid numbers drowsy falling.

Noiseless and still,
O'er star-watched hill,
Beneath the white moon's tender glances,
A host of dreams,
By wind-blown streams,
March on with gleam of silver lances.

A captive thou;
Then, yield thee, now,
While mellow horns are nearer calling;
And ringing bells,
And poppy spells,
Thy senses all in sleep enthralling.

O, hark; O, hear,
My lady, dear,
O'er woods and hills and streamlets flying,
The winding note
Of horns remote,
In softest echo dying—dying.

I had a dream the other night which was like, and yet unlike, the vision of fair women of which a poet once wrote. I dreamed that I sat within a court-room. Before me passed the meanest men and women God ever permitted to live, and upon them I was to pass the verdict as to which should carry off the palm. The scandal-monger came first, he or she who sits like a fly-catcher on a tree, snapping up morsels of news. He or she who is swelled full of conjecture whenever anybody commits an innocent indiscretion, as an owl blinks and ruffles up its feathers when the bobolink sings. He or she who goes about the world like a lean cat after a mouse. He or she who is always looking for clouds in a bright June sky, and slugs in roses and flies in honey. He or she whose heart is made of brass, and whose soul is so small it will take eleven cycles of eternity to develop it to the dimension of a hayseed. I was about to hand this specimen the banner without looking further when a being glided by me with a noiseless tread. She wore felt shoes and a mask. She spoke with the voice of a canary, yet had the talons of a vulture. She wore a stomacher made from the fleece of a lamb, and between her bright red lips were the tusks of a wolf. I recognized her as the hypocrite, the false friend; she who hands over your living bones for your enemies to pick, while you believe she is your champion and your defender. Following her came the man who keeps his horse standing all day with its nose in a nosebag. There was a groan like the sighing of wind in the poplars as he went by. Then came the merciless man who oppresses and torments the helpless and grinds the faces of the poor; and following him I beheld yet another monster—the worst of all in male attire. He came sneaking around a corner, with a smile on his lips and a devil in his eye, seeking to entrap innocent girlhood and unsuspecting womanhood. Then came the woman who gives her children to the care of servants while she goes downtown with a dog in her arms. Then came a lean-faced, weasel-eyed creature with the general expression of a sneak thief. I discovered her to be the representative of that type of women who coaxes her neighbor's hired girl away with promises of better wages. Then came the envious person whose evil passions are kindled like the fires of sheol at the prosperity of others, and who, because his own cup of life holds vinegar, is determined no other shall contain wine. I suddenly awoke without having bestowed the palm on any. Perhaps some of my readers may find it easy to do that for themselves.

Do you know which, of all the sights that confronted me yesterday in my rambles through the rainy weather, I pigeon-holed as the saddest? Not the little white casket, gleaming like the petal of a fallen flower, through the undertaker's rain-streaked window; not the woman with the lack-luster eye and the flippety-floppety petticoats who went by me in the rain silently cursing her bundles and the fact that she was not three-handed; not the poor old cab horse with his nose in a wet bag, and his stomach so tightly buckled in that he couldn't breathe below the fifth rib; not the man out of a job, with his gloveless hands in his pockets, trying to solve the problem of supper; not the little child under convoy of a stern and relentless dragon who yanked it over the crossings by the arm socket; not the starved and absolutely hopeless yellow dog, who sat in a doorway and wondered to himself if there was indeed a canine life that included occasional bones and no kicks; no, not any of these impressed me as the most gruesome of a great city's many sights. As I passed the corner of Washington and Dearborn streets I came face to face with a red-cheeked, wholesome boy of barely twenty years of age. He was leaning upon the arm of an elderly man, and at first I thought him ill, but it took but a second glance to see that he was drunk. Now, I consider that the very saddest sight a great city has to offer. When the old men are wicked there is some comfort in the thought that their day is nearly spent, and their worthless places may be soon filled with a nobler and a better stock, but a drunken and dissolute boy means just what it means for the fruit harvest when the blight gets into the blossom. The gathered apple that rots in the bin is bad enough, but the worm that destroys the fruit in the germ makes greater loss. Be thankful that the grave has taken to its protecting shelter the boy you loved so dearly, and of whom you were so proud, rather than that he should have grown to be a drunkard before his twentieth birthday.

We are each of us missing constant chances to bestow a kindness upon some needy soul for the reason that we dread being imposed upon by a case of causeless complaining. Is it worth while to keep our hearts stolid merely because we may be cheated in the bestowal of a nickel's worth of alms? I think not. You looked up from your work a few minutes ago and saw a little boy not much bigger than your thumb looking through the open doorway. He began at once a sing-song tale of woe about a sick mother and a father out of work—or in his grave, it doesn't much matter. At the same time he held out a paper of cheap pins to tempt a nickel from your store.

"I have no time to bother with such as you," you said, and turned your eyes back to your ledger. But still the boy droned on. You looked at him again and noticed that the small hand that held the pins was well kept and very, very thin. Then your eyes followed the diminutive form down to the feet; they, too, showed signs of somebody's care, although the shoes were shabby and the stockings thin.

"He is not an ordinary little beggar," you

said to yourself. And then your gaze traveled upward again until it met his long-lashed Irish eyes, so full of trouble and of entreaty that they looked like twin Killarney lakes getting ready for rain.

"Poor little chap," you said, "of course I'll buy a paper of pins," and in so doing you stooped over and patted his head, perhaps, or called him "dear," so that he went away with the twin Killarney lakes all ready for a sunburst to follow the rain. That was an opportunity you nearly missed, but it brought a blessing sweeter than a Crawford peach. You didn't want the pins, but the little desolate heart wanted the kind word bestowed along with your nickel, and perhaps its bestowal shall be an impulse toward the light to a soul that cross words and constant refusals had already given a downward trend.

There stands a very young girl at the door of a drug store. She hesitates a moment and enters. "May I sit here and wait for a friend?" she inquires of the dapper clerk. "Certainly," he answers, and places a chair for her near the window.

That girl's father told her last night to have nothing more to do with young Solomon Levi. "He is a worthless fellow," said he, "and I have forbidden him the house." "Very well," said she, and this morning she has made the excuse to go to the grocery for yeast, and is waiting here for the graceless Solomon. By and by he will come, and she will listen to him and form plans for clandestine meetings. My dear, there is a stairway whose top lies in the sunshine, but whose lower steps lead down to endless shadow. Your pretty foot is poising on the upper stair—beware! And yet I think the father has been to blame also. These stern, non-explanatory parents are responsible for much of the ruin wrought in young people's lives. If the old rat would go with the young one now and then to investigate the smell of cheese, his restraining presence would do more good than all the warnings and threats beforehand. Temptations are bound to besiege the girls and bewilder the boys. Don't let us make a pit-fire out of moonshine and forbid every bit of innocent fun and frolic because there is a gayety that takes hold on death. Give the young folks a little more license, mingle with them in many amusements which you have been wont to frown upon, do not be so frightened if their light feet go dancing off the path now and then, and ten to one the end of the journey will be Beulah Land and peace. A good deal less faultfinding and a good deal more sympathy would be better all around.

There is no lot on earth so hard to bear as the lot of wedlock where love has failed. The slave's life is not comparable to it, for the manacles that only bind the hands may be laid aside, but those that fetter the heart not death itself holds the key to loosen. It fairly makes me tremble when I see the thoughtless rush young people make to enter what is by far the most solemn and responsible relation of life. They are like mariners who put to sea in flimsy boats, or like explorers who fit themselves with Prince Albert suits and buttonhole bouquets. Before you get through the voyage, my dears, you will encounter tempests as well as bonnie blue weather, and God pity you when your pleasure craft strikes the first billow, if it was made of caprice and put together with mucilage instead of rivets! As for the explorer and his dress suit, where will he be when the tigers begin to scent him and the air is full of great sorrows and little frets like flying buzzards and cawing crows?

Be an old maid in its most despised significance then; be a grubber and a toiler all the days of your life rather than rush into marriage as a hunted fox flies into a trap. There is some chance for the fox that flies to the hills, and for the bird that soars above the huntsman's aim, but what better off is the fox in the trap or the lark in a cage? There is a love so pure and ennobling that eternity shall not be long enough to cast its blossom, nor death sharp enough to loosen the foundation of its hold. Such love is born in the spirit rather than forced in the hothouse of the senses. It is an impulse toward the stars, a striving toward things that are pure and perfect and true. It grows in the heart as a rose grows in the garden, first a slip, then a leaf and finally the perfect blossom. No rose ever put forth a flower first, and then bethought itself of rooting and budding. Pray, dear girls, that this love may come to you rather than its poor prototype, so current in a world of shams and pretenses, whose luster corrodes with daily usage and turns to pewter in your grasp.

Once there was an old woman who died and went to glory. Now a great many old women have died and gone the same way, but this one was very tired and very glad to go. She had worked hard ever since she could handle a broom or flirt a duster. She had probably washed about 91,956,045 dishes in her life, had baked something less than a million of pies, and turned out anywhere between a quarter to half a million loaves of bread, to say nothing of biscuits. These figures are steep, but I am writing under the invigorating impulse of the grip! She had darned socks and hemmed towels and patched old pantaloon-seats between times, until her fingers were callous as agate. She had borne and reared lots of children and tended to their myriad wants. For forty-seven years she had done a big washing every week, and laundried more collars than a Canada thistle has seed-pods. At last she died. The tired old body burst its withered husk and let the flower free. The rusty old cage flew open and out went the bird. And when they buried her I suppose they were foolish enough to shed tears and put on mourning! As well expect all the birds to wear crape when dawn sets out its primrose-pot on the ledge of the eastern sky! But one friend of quicker perception than the rest, I am told, placed the following inscription on the tired old woman's gravestone:

Here lies a poor woman who always was tired,
For she lived in a world where much was required.
"Weep not for me, friends," she said, "for I'm going
Where there'll be neither washing, nor baking, nor sewing;
Then weep not for me; if death must us sever,
Rejoice that I'm going to do nothing forever."

There is just one thing in the latter part of the nineteenth century that never fails to bring success, and that is assurance. If you are going to make yourself known it is no longer the thing to quietly pass out a visiting card—you must advance with a trumpet and blow a brazen blast to shake the stars.

The time has gone by when self-advancement can be gained by modest and unassuming methods. To stand with a lifted hat and solicit a hearing savors of mendicancy and an humble spirit. The easily abashed and the diffident may starve in a garret, or go die on the highways—there is no chance for them in the jostling rush of life. The gilded circus chariot, with a full brass band and a plump goddess distributing circulars, is what takes the popular heart by storm. Your silent entry into town, depending upon the merits of your wares to gain an audience or work up a custom, is chimerical and obsolete. We no longer sit in the shadow and play flutes; we mount a pine platform and blow on a trombone, and in that way we draw a crowd, and that is what we live for. Who are the women who succeed in business ventures of any sort? Mostly the mannish, bold, aggressive amazons who are unmindful of rebuffs and impervious to contempt. Who are the men who wear diamonds and live easy lives? Largely the politicians who have made their reputation in bar-room rostrums and among sharpers. Oh, for a wind to blow us forward a hundred years out of this age of sordid self-seeking and impudent assertiveness into something larger and sweeter and finer. Give us less yeast in our bread and more substance; fill our cups with wine rather than froth, and for sweet pity's sake hang up the great American trumpet and let "silence, like a poultice, come to heal the blows of sound."

Every day, for months, as I have taken my morning ride to town I have noticed a dog who bounds forth from a dooryard that overlooks the busy highway of the steed of steam and barks himself weak at the rushing trains. He really accomplishes nothing, but do you suppose you could convince his canine brain that he was not at once a reproach and a terror to the numerous trains that disturb his rest? He reminds me of certain people we meet all the way through life. They bark at trains continually while the Lord prolongs their breath, and the faster the train and the more it carries the louder they bark. They fondly imagine that the voice of their ranting protest accomplishes a purpose in the world. They are always barking at capital and at rich men and at corporations. They bark at people of courteous manners, and all the ways and customs of polite and gentle society, with fierce and futile yelpings. They bark at the swift advancement of the world from ignorance to enlightenment, from superstition to liberalism. They bark at the churches because they are on a train that has side-tracked Calvin. They bark at polite young men who wear clean linen, and call them dudes; they bark at women who have one or two ideas outside of fashionable folly and inane conventionalism, and call them cranks; they bark at everything on wheels, where wheels typify strength and achievement. They will go on barking, too, while the world finds room and maintains patience for them and their barking.

I think I have said before that I loathe meek people. But even if I have I am going to say it again. Your half-wits who sit and turn first one cheek and then the other to be slapped are not the sort for me. The man or woman, boy or girl, child or otherwise, that will endure direct insult day after day without resenting it ought to sell themselves at so much a pint for illuminating oil—that is all they are good for. I love a fighter, provided he foils gracefully and does not snatch out his sword in every brawling and unworthy cause. In the defense of woman, in the cause of honor, purity and truth; in battle against sordidness, and greed, and a lying tongue, let your blade flash like summer rain and your white plume outdistance the plume of Navarre! For God and mother, justice and honor, self-respect and the approval of our own conscience, let us go forward then with a chip, if need be, on each shoulder and a standard copy of the celestial army tactics in our side pocket! The Lord loves a good many things, cheerful givers and self-sacrificing widows with their mites, merciful men and sweet and noble women, but most of all, I think, he loves a valiant fighter in the cause of right.

Now it came to pass that there dwelt in a certain city of the land of the great lakes a woman called Lydia, sister to Simon, the shipwright. And Lydia, being comely and fair to look upon, was sought in marriage by one John, a dealer in spices and fine teas. And the years of their wedlock having outnumbered the fingers upon a man's two hands, it came to pass that they dwelt together in exceeding prosperity in a town near by the blue waters of a mighty lake.

And Heaven sent unto them children to the number of three, so that their hearts were exceeding glad, and the cords of their habitation were stretched from year to year. And it came to pass that the home in which they lived was spacious and full of salubrious air. Their beds, also, were of curled hair, and all their bed-springs of beaten steel. And bath-rooms made glad the heart of the dust-laden when summer dwelt in the land. Also there were cunningly devised screens of fine wire in all the windows, so that the marauding fly and the pestilential mosquito might not enter.

And the flesh increased from year to year upon the bones of Lydia and the children that heaven sent her, while they remained in the home that John, the tea merchant, had given them.

But it came to pass that the neighbors of the woman Lydia closed up the shutters of their dwellings, and one by one stole from town when the heat descended upon the land.

Then spake Lydia unto John, the vender of spices and fine teas, saying:

"Arise, let us go hence and dwell within a farm-house, where the children may leap together in the sweet-smelling hay, and I may comfort myself with flagons of cream."

But John, being a man among men, and accounted somewhat wise withal, would have restrained Lydia, saying: "Not so; for verily I say unto you, comfort abideth not in the dwelling of the farmer, neither does joy linger in the shadow of his doorway."

Now Lydia, being president of a Woman's Club and reputed of knowledge beyond the generality of womankind, would not listen, but beat her hands together, crying: "I prithee hold thy peace, for behold, I and the children heaven sent me will depart hence by to-morrow's chariot of steam, and will make our home with the gentle farmer and his sweet-breathed kine."

So John, being loth to war with the tongue, albeit he was heavy-hearted and walked with a bent head, purchased tickets for Lydia and the children heaven had given her.

And it came to pass that they left town by the train which men call "the limited."

Now the way of that train through the land is like unto the way of a ship at sea, or of a strong eagle that never wearieth. And the sufferings of Lydia were such that she sought relief in peppermint and found it not.

And the babes by reason of the swiftness with which they traversed a crooked land, were made ill and languished like sea-sick rangers of the deep.

Yet, after many hours, their torment abated not, so that, reaching their destination, the bodies of Lydia and her children were removed in a hack and hurried to an inn that was built near by.

And in the inn where they were fain to tarry until strength should be given them for further journeying, it chanced that a young babe lay sorely stricken with the whooping-cough.

Now, when Lydia knew this, her heart fainted with fear, and she prophesied evil.

For well she knew that her own babes had not had the disease, and that the time of their prostration was at hand.

So Lydia, being president of a Woman's

Club, and accounted without a peer in the gift of words, sent for the keeper of the inn, that she might rebuke him.

And she opened her mouth impulsively and questioned him saying: "Why broughtest thou me and the children heaven gave me into thine inn knowing that contagious disease lurked within its gates?"

And the keeper of the inn shot out the lip at her and was undismayed.

And he cried, "Go to! And what wouldst thou of a public house? Thou talkest like one with little sense!"

And it came to pass that Lydia and her children departed thence by stage and sought the farm-house. And, arriving there, they would have laid themselves down to rest, being sorely bruised by reason of protracted stage-riding.

But the beds were made of straw and corded underneath with ropes. So that lying upon them caused the children to roar loudly, and they found rest from their lamentations, four in a bed, on the bosom of Lydia.

And, supper being served, it consisted of tinted warm water and gooseberries sweetened with brown sugar.

Now Lydia, by reason of her connection with the club, was enabled to speak boldly, and she called for cream.

But the wife of the farmer made answer, saying, "We have none."

And Lydia spoke yet again, saying, "Why, O woman of many wiles, hast thou no cream?"

And the woman made way with an insect that swam gaily in a pitcher of azure milk, and said gently, "Because we sell it to a neighboring dairy."

And Lydia said nothing, but remembering the words of John, the tea-merchant, wept silently.

And it came to pass that next morning the children went forth to leap in the hay.

And the farmer led them firmly away from the hay-mow by the tip of the ear, saying, "I allow no children to spoil my fodder."

And the morning of the second day, the woman Lydia, being starved for nutritious food, wended her way with her babes across a stretch of pasture land in search of wild blackberries.

And a beast, whose voice was baritone and whose approach was like the approach of a Kansas cyclone, bore down upon her and the children heaven had given her, while yet they were midway in the meadow. Now only by leaping could they save themselves.

And it came to pass that they leaped mightily and flung themselves over a five-barred fence.

And a snake made free with the draperies of Lydia, so that her hair whitened with fear, and between the beast with the baritone voice and the serpent she knew not which way to turn.

And the morning of the third day she wrote to John, the tea-merchant, saying only:

"My darling—Meet the first train that returns from this place to the dear city by the lake, for behold! I and the children heaven sent me are on our homeward way!"

IMPATIENCE.

A sweet little crocus came up through the mold,
And hugged round her shoulders her mantle of
    gold,
While tears of distress fringed her delicate eye,
Like rain drops that start from a showery sky.

Rosemary and Rue.

"Where, pray, are those laggards, the violets blue?
The roses and lilies and daffodils too?
I really think it's a shame and a sin
This waiting so long for the spring to begin.

"The first day of April and only one bird
Since I lifted my head has uttered a word!
And search as I may all over the meadow
Not even a cowslip has shown its bright head, O-

"Misery me! Sure there's no use in waiting,
For something, no doubt, is the summer belating;
So I'll go back to bed, put on my lace night cap,
And snatch, for a fortnight, a nice little cat-nap!"

Down went little Gold-head, back to her pillow;
When, all in a twinkling, up over the hill, O,
The wind-flower host, with rose-tinted banners,
Marched into the world; Queen Summer's fore-runners.

Her rose maids of honor, in filmiest laces,
Loitered and lingered in shy woodland places;
And white-vested lilies were ever at prayer;
Their vespers, the perfume that sweetened the air.

The apple trees blushed into delicate splendor;
The blue birds hung over in ecstasy tender,
While the gold powdered bee with helmet all dusty
Kept watch over the flowers, a sentinel trusty.

The robin sang love to his shy little sweetheart;
The orioles lashed their nests in the tree top;
The willows drooped low over swift water courses,
And murmuring brooks started fresh from their sources.

But down in the gloom, on her dream-haunted pillow,
As pale and as cold as the moon on the billow,
Forgot and unmissed by bird and by blossom,
The crocus slept sound in the earth's faithful bosom.

When at last she awoke, the spring had been banished,
Her forerunner flowers from the hillside had vanished.
And all of the bees had turned into stock brokers.
And even the birds had changed into croakers.

'Tis only by waiting we find our fruition;
To learn how to wait is a needed tuition.
The faint-hearted people who go to sleep fretting,
Will wake up at last too late for the getting.

If there is anything more utterly desolate than a poorly-conducted farm, preserve me from it. There is an ideal farm familiar to the writers of pretty tales, where everything is kept in apple-pie order throughout the year, and where one can walk broadcast, so to speak, in a spick and span white gown without attracting so much as the shadow of a shade of minutest defilement. We have seen pictures of such farms wherein sleek cattle stood around knee-deep in dewy clover, or lay serenely on polished hillsides, or meandered dreamily by crystal streams; wherein pale pink farm-houses with green gables and yellow piazzas, fairly scintillated from behind decorous foliage, and peacocks, with tails nearly as long as the Mississippi River, posed on the gate-posts; wherein neat little boys in variegated trousers rode prancing chargers down blooming lanes, and correct little girls in ruffled underclothing fed well-mannered chickens from morning till night. But the actual farm of the remote rural districts is about as much like its ideal picture as Esau was like a modern dude. Not long ago somebody suggested that I go and board for a fortnight at a farmhouse. "You will have perfect rest," said my friend, "and that is what you need." So I went, and rather than again undergo the torments of the five days spent in that restful (?) spot I think I would cheerfully hire out with a Siberian chain-gang. In the first place there was no such a thing as rest possible after the first glimmer of each day's dawn. Every rooster on the farm, and there were millions of them, was up "for keeps" long before sunrise. Their united chorus smote the skies. One might as well have tried to sleep through Gettysburg's battle. A score or so of bereaved cows lamented all night for their murdered babies, and a couple of donkeys, kept purely for ornamental purposes, made sounds every half hour or so that turned my hair snow white with terror. After breakfast each day I used to walk down the hill and fish for pickerel in a river that had no current, and looked discouraged. "Walked," did I say? Nay, there was nothing so decorous as a walk possible down the slippery, stony descent which led to the haunts of the pickerel. When I didn't hurl myself down that hill, I slid down, and between the two methods I wrecked both muscle and shoe leather. The latter part of the way led through a pasture devoted to several cows and a bull. As I am more afraid of the latter than of death and all his cohorts, my morning walks ended in heart failures and had to be abandoned. Occasionally I would take a book and go out and sit in my hammock. Then the large roosters, each one of them at least seven feet tall and highly ruffled about the legs, would come around and look at me, so that I would have to go into the house to hide my embarrassment. I know of nothing harder to endure than the stare of a Brahma fowl, especially if one is a bit nervous and overworked. Nervous prostration has sprung from lighter causes.

Nothing happened while I was at the farm but meal time, and the intervals were so long between those episodes that I used to wonder daily at my own mission subsequent to the farm-life as one gropes for pre-historic clues. There was a man about the premises who walked to and from the village twice a day with a large brown jug. When I asked at different times what he fetched in the jug, not because I wanted to know, but merely to find a topic of conversation, I was successively told that it was "kerosene," "maple molasses," "buttermilk," and "vinegar." I wish I knew if I was told the truth every time, or if somebody tried to impose upon me merely because I was town-bred.

Occasionally we took rides over stony trails where boulders and ruts marked the way, and only the creaking of our bones broke the primeval silence. These rides were supposed to be part of the generous plan of contemplated rest, but a few more of them would have resulted in the rest from which there is no awaking. No, my dear, I am an ardent lover of the country, and I love it as the epicure loves a good dinner, or the musician loves music, but I will take it, please, without the accessories of a poorly-kept hoosier farm. I do not yearn for the defilements of a barn-yard that is never cleansed, nor for the frolicsomeness of pigs that wander at their own sweet will, nor for the clamor of aggressively alert poultry, nor for piscatorial delights. I love the country as God made it before greed and gain and all the abominations of man entered into and spoiled it. I love it clean and wholesome and sweet, as it was turned out of the workshop; its streams untainted, and their banks unbereft of beautiful trees; its hills still covered with verdure, and its winds uncontaminated with the scent of defiling drains and waterways.

I have seen him! Actually seen him! Shall I say the coming man? No, rather let us call him the vanished type, the stalwart, full-blooded, glorious "might have been" of nature. Not an exotic, but the indigenous growth of a soil fed by breeze and sun. No earmuffs about him; no cringing withdrawal into mufflers before the advance of winter blasts. No cowardly retreat into furry overcoats, mittens and gum shoes.

"Amber," said a fellow traveler the other day, "yonder is a man after your own heart. He has not worn an overcoat or heavyweight flannels for six years. He never buttons up his coat save when it rains. What do you think of him?"

"Think of him!" said I; "were it not for a lingering regard for the conventionalities, I should walk right over to that man and say: 'Sir, I thank you for the sight of a man —not a human lily bud! You have struck the right way of living, and you will be a hale and handsome man when the enfeebled race that surrounds you have toddled into the consumptive's grave or are sneezing upon their catarrhal pilgrimage to the tomb." The man was worth looking at, hale and hearty, his chest like the convex curve of a barrel, his eye like a falcon's.

"But," said my friend, "were I to throw aside my overcoat and go forth unprotected this freezing weather, the exposure would surely kill me!"

"No doubt it would," was my cheerful reply. "There are always a host to die before any reform is achieved or victory accomplished. You have coddled yourself so long between blankets and absorbed red-hot furnace heat until you haven't the stamina of an aspen leaf. Take a hot-house flower out of doors and it soon wilts. But mark the beautiful Edelweiss of the Alps—it thrives in the pure breath of eternal snow." But what is the use of talking? Although my tongue became a golden bell and my pen a gleaming flame, I could never convince you, my dear old, shivery, shaky public, of the advantage of fresh air and plenty of it, and the advisability of a generous cultivation of nature and her free gifts. As well expect to be nourished by looking at your food through an opera glass as hope to be strong and stalwart upon a homeopathic allowance of pure air and sunshine, or in spite of the devices you plan to shut yourself away and hermetically seal your body, as it were, from the sweet, health-giving influence of sun and wind and frost. Just stop a moment before you turn away from this subject, my dear, and hear a little story. I know the subject is a bore and that I am a crank, but listen. Once there was a grand beneficent power—call it God if you will—who planned a spot wherein to place some atom which he had shaped out of dust and vivified with a spark of his own life. He looked about a little, we will imagine, and finally settled upon a garden wherein to place these precious pensioners on his care. A roofless, wall-less spot full of draughts and dew, breezes and blossoms. He filled it with birds and carpeted it with grass, set rivulets running through it for "water works" and sunbeams and starbeams for "electric light" plants, etc. That is all I have to say. Like the Mother Morey legend my story is done before it is scarcely begun. But ask yourself the question, Why didn't God put his well-beloved models of the forthcoming race into a more sheltered place if there was so much danger in fresh air, draughts and chilly weather? Why didn't he seal them up behind double windows in an airless, sunless, hot and unhealthful home where the dear things could keep warm? Because he was God and knew everything, and not man and knew nothing.

Well, the old ship Time has put into port again to take on a new cargo of good resolutions, earnest resolves and patented schemes, before setting sail for the shores of a distant future. Ten to one she goes to pieces on the breakers before ever sighting land again, and a hundred to ninety-nine her cargo is thrown overboard before she reaches mid-sea. The channel is narrow and the rocks lie thick as peas in a marrowfat pod, and many more bales of choice merchandise find the bottom of the sea each year than are ever delivered to the good angel consignee. "I am going to be the best girl in all the world," says the poor little Captain on New Year's eve. Behold! the hours have not swung around the diurnal circle before there is a wild onslaught from shadowland, and the brave captain is left wounded on the field. Only a tender hand and tireless patience can set her on her feet again.

"I will eschew debt as I would poison, and starve before I will commit an indiscretion," cries the Doctor as he sets sail for the untried sea. Within the first watch he hauls down his colors from the mast head, captured by a pirate extravagance.

"I will be gentle of speech and courteous and sweet to all!" says the Young Person, and gayly steers for the open channel. Midway she encounters a rock of annoyance and the air is stormy with irritable words that fly and beat like stinging rain. Ah, well, my dear, thank the good Lord there are life-saving stations all along the shore, and no wreck was ever yet so hopeless but Infinite Love could set it afloat again.

"There is just one person born who has a right to this thoroughfare, and that is I!" muses the woman with the umbrella as she walks the crowded streets on a rainy day. "I am in possession of that part of the universe immediately contiguous to the spot on which I stand, and I shall make myself just as much of a nuisance as I choose. I shall jab out your eyes, and knock off your hat, and clip your ears, and stab your back with my umbrella tip just as often and as violently as I choose. I shall run into you from behind, and bump into you, and knock you down if I so desire, and none shall say me nay. I am not very tall, but all the better for my plans if I am not. If I were of the same height as you I should not be able to take you under the hat-brim as I do, and jab you in the nostril as I pass. If I choose to cut criss-cross through a crowd, who shall forbid me, being a woman? I can be just as rude and just as mean as I want to be, and who is going to hinder, so long as I wear a gown and call myself a lady? If I were a man and manifested the reckless thirst for universal carnage that I do you would call the patrol and bear me away to the lock-up; but being a poor little, innocent woman I have it all my own way."

I know a wife who is waiting, safe and sound in her father's home, for her young husband to earn the money single-handed to make a home worthy of her acceptance. She makes me think of the first mate of a ship who should stay on shore until the captain tested the ability of his vessel to weather the storm. Back to your ship, you cowardly one! If the boat goes down, go down with it, but do not count yourself worthy of any fair weather you did not help to gain! A woman who will do all she can to win a man's love merely for the profit his purse is going to be to her, and will desert him when the cash runs low, is a bad woman and carries a bad heart in her bosom. Why, you are never really wedded until you have had dark days together. What earthly purpose would a cable serve that never was tested by a weight? Of what use is the tie that binds wedded hearts together if like a filament of floss it parts when the strain is brought to bear upon it? It is not when you are young, my dear, when the skies are blue and every wayside weed flaunts a summer blossom, that the story of your life is recorded. It is when "Darby and Joan" are faded and wasted and old, when poverty has nipped the roses, when trouble and want and care have flown like uncanny birds over their heads (but never yet nested in their hearts, thank God!), that the completed chronicle of their lives furnishes the record over which approving heaven smiles and weeps.

There is one thing I learn day by day in my strollings about town, and that is that nobody is going to give me dollar values for half-dollar equivalents. In these days when the best of folks go mad on bargains we seem to think it is an easy thing to get something for nothing, but I have yet to see the day when we can. There are cheap restaurants where they serve you roast turkey for a quarter, but don't fool yourself! It is not the same kind of bird they serve in a high-class place for a dollar. You look at your check when you come out from an economical kitchen with a feeling of glee that you have got so much for so little. But how about the flavor that lingers in your mouth? How about the display of pine toothpicks and spotted linen? How about the finger-marked drinking glasses and damp napkins? No, no; poor as I am I would rather pay my dollar and get a dollar's worth of cleanliness and daintiness and flavor than save seventy-five cents and do without them. Sure as you live and sure as the world is operated on a self-accommodative basis, you never will get a first-water diamond without you pay first-water diamond equivalents.

The other day there was a little girl, scarce 16 years of age, who started away for the first time from home and mother. She was brave and gay in a new suit, new boots and a new hat with a feather the color of a linnet's wing. She carried a bunch of the loveliest sweet peas at her dainty waist and on her face there played a sunburst of smiles. She had not been five hours in the place appointed her to visit when her mother received the following letter:

"My Precious Mamma: I am writing this in my room before I am called to breakfast. None but God can know what I suffer! Not until I am in your arms once more will you know what I am going through! If you love me let me come home. Don't tell anyone, but let me come if you love me! Don't send the shoes—I shall not need them—but let me come home! Think what I must suffer so far away from you. I shall sell my ring and buy a ticket if you do not telegraph that I may come!"

And as I read the pathetic letter between my smiles and tears I thought to myself, is there anything on earth so hard to bear as homesickness—first homesickness, when the heart is new to sorrow? I would rather have any disease the laboratory of evil keeps in stock than one pang of what that little girl was suffering when she penciled that letter.

Around in a picture store on one of the avenues I chanced upon a painting that attracted not only myself, but a crowd of people from the street. It represented a lion's cage barred with heavy barriers of iron. On the floor of the den is the figure of a beautiful girl stretched in a deathlike swoon. There are orange blossoms in her hair, and the flush on her cheek has had no time to fade. Crouched by her side, one great paw on her breast and another at her waist, is a wrathful lion whose evident intention is to tear his victim into bonbon fragments. I wish somebody would explain that picture to me. I am tired conjecturing how the bride strayed into the lion's quarters, and where her husband was that he shouldn't be taking better care of her, and why there was nobody on hand to help at this critical moment portrayed on the canvas. Young married women are not supposed to be visiting zoological gardens when they ought to be changing their white satin favors for their traveling gowns. The picture seems a puzzler to all who watch it, and as the crowd is great the confusion of wits is catching.

THE TRYST.

Where a woodland path, like a silver line,
    Winds by a woodland river,
And half in shadow, and half in shine,
    The alders lean and shiver,
Where a forest bird has built him a nest
    Low in the springing grasses,
And all the day long, with her wings at rest,
    His mate the slow time passes;

Where a flood of gold through the forest dim
    Tells when the noon is strongest,

And a purple fringe on the forest's rim
  Proclaims when the shades are longest;
Where the dawn is only known from the night
  By the birds that sing their sweetest,
And the twilight hush from the morning light
  By the peace that is then completest;

Where only the flood of silvery haze
  Shall tell that the moon is risen,
When down from the sky, like a meteor blaze,
  Shall flutter her snow-white ribbon,—
I will meet you there, my lady love sweet,
  When the weary world is sleeping,
And the frets of the day, that tireless beat,
  Are hushed in the night's close keeping;

Not missing the world—by the world un-
  missed—
  We two shall wander together,
And whether we chided, or whether we kissed,
  There'll be none to forget or remember;
And when at the last asleep you shall fall,
  By the shore of the musical river,
Of the crimson leaves I will weave you a pall,
  And kiss you good-by, love, forever.

But the stars up above, and the waters below,
  Shall sing of us, over and over;
Of the tryst that we kept in the years long ago,
  In the woods by the beautiful river.

www.ingramcontent.com/pod-product-compliance
Lightning Source LLC
Chambersburg PA
CBHW032042230426
43672CB00009B/1433